COMMENTARY ON

COME AND TAKE IT

"A foreboding and revealing chronicle of a year that created one of the most radically anarchist provocations in the history of the amoral Internet."

—Andy Greenberg, author of *This Machine Kills Secrets*

"A manifesto about the right to bear arms and the freedom of ideas . . . chilling."

—*Esquire*

"A self-styled anarchist serves up a troubling vision."

—*Kirkus Reviews*

"A rollicking, almost stream-of-consciousness account."

—*The Wall Street Journal*

"In the season of Trump, it feels like a warning of madness and violence to come."

—*The Economist*

COME AND TAKE IT

The Gun Printer's Guide to Thinking Free

Cody Wilson

G
GALLERY BOOKS
New York   London   Toronto   Sydney   New Delhi

G

Gallery Books
An Imprint of Simon & Schuster, Inc.
1230 Avenue of the Americas
New York, NY 10020

Certain names have been changed.

First Gallery Books paperback edition June 2017

GALLERY BOOKS and colophon are registered trademarks of Simon & Schuster, Inc.

For information about special discounts for bulk purchases,
please contact Simon & Schuster Special Sales at 1-866-506-1949
or business@simonandschuster.com.

The Simon & Schuster Speakers Bureau can bring authors to your live event.
For more information or to book an event contact the Simon & Schuster Speakers Bureau at 1-866-248-3049 or visit our website at www.simonspeakers.com.

Interior design by Davina Mock-Maniscalco

Manufactured in the United States of America

10 9 8 7 6 5 4 3 2 1

Library of Congress Cataloging-in-Publication Data
Names: Wilson, Cody, author.
Title: Come and take it : the gun printer's guide to thinking free / Cody Wilson.
Description: New York : Gallery Books, [2016]
Identifiers: LCCN 2015044486
Subjects: LCSH: Wilson, Cody. | Firearms ownership—United States. | Firearms—Law and legislation—United States. | Firearms—Design and construction. | Three-dimensional printing.
Classification: LCC HV7436 .W545 2016 | DDC 323.4/3—dc23 LC record available at http://lccn.loc.gov/2015044486

ISBN 978-1-4767-7826-6
ISBN 978-1-4767-7827-3 (pbk)
ISBN 978-1-4767-7828-0 (ebook)

For my parents, Dennis and Cecelia
and
To the memory of my grandfather, Harold B. Wilson

There is much more to be hoped for in an excess of information or of weapons than in the restriction of information or arms control.

—Jean Baudrillard

CONTENTS

PROLOGUE

WikiLeaks, Solid Imaging, and Open Source
xi

PART I

Wiki Weapon
1

PART II

Ministry of Defense
25

PART III

The Gun Printer
45

PART IV

Terror
79

PART V

Danger
99

PART VI

Jarhead Angel
125

PART VII

John
147

PART VIII

Modern Politics
177

PART IX

Dropping the Liberator
197

PART X

Old Street
219

PART XI

Who Does What to Whom
231

PART XII

Wine-Dark
245

PART XIII

Undetectable
261

PART XIV

REDACTED
283

EPILOGUE

Nine Months of Night
299

WikiLeaks, Solid Imaging, and Open Source

At high summer, we gathered in Little Rock at the Peabody. By the evening the hotel's signature ducks—four hens and a drake—would have already completed their twice-daily march from the rooftop penthouse to the lobby fountain, where they fluttered and splashed.

In a few more months the Southern charm would be wrung from the place: no more mallards in the elevator. But back then, in the summer of 2012, we basked in the final flickering of it all. We drank to the uneasiness in culture.

Music, voices, and the sounds of the running fountain danced about the marbled, open floors. Golden light filled the huge recesses above and around the lobby bar, ringed by six great pillars. The hotel opened directly onto Markham Street and the walking crowds on the Old Statehouse plaza. I lured any who might listen to this marvelous set piece with the grandest exhortations—*Would you be remembered?*—and here made a ritual of holding a fiendish court.

At one of these twilight salons sat Chris Hancock, an old classmate of mine, his tangled black hair brushed from his face. He had brought a friend.

"You remember WikiLeaks!" I insisted to them both. "Do you recall the insurance files?"

"WikiLeaks sends everything they've got out to the public in advance. It's all published and torrented but protected from reading by some long password, right?" Chris answered.

"Exactly," I said, losing the word on my breath. "And in the event the states move in for some final shutdown, only then do they release the password. The copies were already distributed. The damage sits waiting to be done. Maybe the files had been seeded for months, maybe years. You can't pull them all down. The threat is credible because everyone has a computer. Every computer is always already on the Internet."

"Peer-to-peer technology gives you leverage, sure. So, what are you saying?"

"What I'm saying is you can leak more than emails and cables. There are new machines—networked, material printers. They use complex and evolving materials. Into this budding universe of digital production . . . *you leak a gun.*"

I liked to watch the realization come to people in stages. It had been no different with Chris. Except on this night he made a conceptual leap.

"A Wiki Weapon," he mused, looking down at the square candle on our table.

And I admit I was a little stunned by the words. Alarmed, even, that the clever coinage was a sign I still didn't understand the significance of the proposition after these months. They made me jealous too.

Chris's friend looked at both of us then, his face flushed with the chill of true and unwelcome surprise. And I whispered it:

"We are the heartworms of history."

———————

The eminent science-fiction writer Arthur C. Clarke's Third Law states: "Any sufficiently advanced technology is indistinguishable from magic." Although 3D printing may seem like magic, it came from very practical beginnings.

A man named Chuck Hull first demonstrated "solid imaging" in the lab in 1984. He translated a digital design into a set of coordinates able to be translated to an ultraviolet beam aimed at a vat of liquid photopolymer. As the light traced lines upon the surface of this bath, the exposed lines cured and solidified.

After a cross section of the design was drawn, the laser traced another section to build another layer. Chuck says he woke his wife in the night to show her his first true part. He patented the technology and co-founded a company to sell it by the name of 3D Systems.

In the late eighties, Scott Crump pioneered a method for solid imaging based on the controlled layering of thermoplastic through a filament feed. The "Eureka!" story goes that he was inspired by his use of a hot-glue gun one afternoon.

Around the same time, in 1984, Richard Stallman, a programmer from Harvard and MIT, was on a mission to offer computer users something entirely different: "free software." "The word 'free' in our name does not refer to price," he wrote in 1986. "It refers to freedom." Users would be given the freedom to copy a program and redistribute it to their neighbors. And they would be able to change a program so that they could control it. This meant that the source code for the program would be publicly available.

The term *open source* came from a working group in California responding to a monumental act by Netscape, who decided to offer their browser as free software to the public in 1998. Free and open-source software can now be found everywhere you look. Names like Linux, Python, Apache, Perl, and perhaps even Bitcoin may not mean much to you, but you likely use devices or applications based upon these open-source softwares every day of your life.

I consider myself lucky to have been attending the University of Texas at Austin when we began the work that would lead to the 3D printed pistol. The university was at the forefront of developing 3D printing techniques in the 1980s, and in the years since I began the project, I've been regularly surprised by its academic and commercial contributions to the technologies I was exploring—not to mention the contributions of the state of Texas as a whole.

Over the years I've picked through the old papers on the printing innovations, usually with an eye for the personalities of the early authors and industry players. When I read Dr. Paul Jacobs's work from the early nineties, what stood out to me most was his American optimism. He believed the technology was and would be a great boon to American enterprise.

So, 3D printing has been around for a while. But the consumer at large mostly started hearing about it only in the last several years. Why?

A New York startup named Makerbot brought to market the first successful line of retail 3D printers in 2011. If the success of our printed pistol was not your introduction to the idea of 3D printing, it was most likely Makerbot in 2012 and 2013 that caught your attention: the company's rise and disgraceful fall have been almost totally responsible for shaping the public's perceptions and expectations of 3D printing. And here we are . . .

I knew almost none of this when I began the work of Defense Distributed.

People have asked me why we printed a gun. Why I set out to print a handgun instead of, say, a heart valve. But our story doesn't begin with the question put that way. In private conversation, when I try to answer the question *why*, I like to remind people what was said about our pistol (and by whom) after it was released. For example, Eric Schmidt, State capitalist extraordinaire, pronounced the release of the gun's files a "moral crime." I'll point to the swift action by the US State Department to swallow up the gun's files into the very matrix of information control the project was designed to attack. Or I'll mention the attempts of foreign governments, mostly Western, to surveil or license their citizens' use of digital fabrication devices.

I believe the printed pistol lays bare Western ethical ideology and gets to the heart of the question of the political. Your politics will inform what you think about our actions, but you may feel differently about the potential of powerful, free, and open-source software and intellectual property after you've read this book.

Our story starts with Benjamin Denio calling me on the phone late into my second semester of law school in Austin. He merely offered idle speculation about the future of the firearm.

I was simply seduced by the idea and the wilderness to which it would bring me.

PART I

Wiki Weapon

Benjamin Denio was the first person socially constructed for me wholly by Facebook. That's what I remember thinking. Awkwardly squatting in the pale light in my tiny kitchen, staring at the dusty linoleum, I leaned my head into the cabinet and thought about how I hadn't even met the man on the other end of the line. His Facebook, for what that was worth, told me he enjoyed Clausewitz, dank memes, and the more terrifying of the DARPA ventures. In his posts he wildly seethed against the local government in Little Rock and the deniers of climate change. Perhaps he meant it. Perhaps he just wanted better web ads.

If no alarm sounded in some room in Virginia upon our first contact, I trust the matter has been referred to the relevant committee.

Ben and I had attended the same university in Arkansas, it turned out. I recalled seeing him at a campus meeting called by Kenny Grand, the leader of the student United Leftist Front. Kenny's large, anachronistic persona was a stand-in for the bigger ideas most of the ULF couldn't quite articulate. I believe he was celebrated as a representation, living proof that there were Ideas somewhere above Arkansan experience, like Labor and the Revolution. That men once had historical passions, and that they, being dead, yet speaketh. He sat cross-legged in the corners of many meetings like this one, speaking with certainty, and that was enough. Something you could point to. Kenny understood. But then we prefer signs to the things signified.

At this particular meeting, the students of the ULF protested the university police's acquisition of assault rifles, and the administration had a brilliant line: "They were a private gift, you see, and it would be rude to return them. Besides, it's not like you're paying for them." We were sullen. This was a gift power could return but would not. But there were things we hadn't then considered. There are some gifts that power *cannot* give back, even if it would like to.

Ben and I had been thinking in tune then. And I knew we were now. By our slowly budding virtual association, I'd discovered he was both a practicing Buddhist and an urban guerrilla. He carried on like he'd be among those first few men to bolt a gun to the back of a pickup truck and head screaming for the wastes should things go sideways. And like me, he found that ours was not a world in need of protection from the threat of too much terrorism. We were instead terrorized by the threat of too much protection. I'd been talking to him on the phone on and off for over six months now.

Bent over and letting my hunger gnaw at me, I stared through the grimy floor while I took in his broken, digital voice. Ben loved the way Moscow was playing spoiler in Syria. He was at his place in Little Rock going on about the latest Russian military dogmata. "The future is hybrid warfare," he told me.

Ben was terribly immersed in the lore and technology of the Soviet period and thereafter. He frequently mixed his historical analysis with stories from his time playing video games like *Hearts of Iron* and *Wargame*, a real-time strategy game in which you could build and battle with your own NATO or Warsaw Pact armies, fighting against others online. As we spoke, I supposed the vague beeps I heard were some kind of combat notice.

I wasn't a gamer myself, but I understood the impulse, especially with historical games—the desire to not just relive great moments but to thereby relive great ideas. His combination of Buddhism and bellicosity made Ben's incongruence at times conspicuous. But then so was my own. And any man worth knowing is a man at war with himself.

As it often did, the subject of our call turned to the technical. "A lot of people dismiss 'good enough' technology, man. Perfect is the enemy of good enough, right?"

I was half listening to Ben run off on his tangent while I thought, with some regret, about the project the two of us had worked at the year before. Super PACs after 2010 had become a public issue and proliferated wildly. We, but then I should say I, wanted to make one that was toxic in nature. Pick House races with the least amount of spending, then buy up as much of the airwaves as possible for terrible ads.

Turn people completely off to the electoral and political process. It was a fun thought experiment. I'd always had the trickster sensibility and this approach appealed to that part of me. Play by the rules, but ruin the game to show the absurdity of it all.

Ben and I had come to the same conclusions regarding super PACs and believed they eventually would become more heavily funded than the traditional political parties. Maybe they'd become huge, king-making interest groups in their own right. Single-issue media attack machines. You could see Karl Rove and the Koch brothers operating them like niche extensions of the wider GOP apparatus. There would be success there, sure, but we imagined a more hybridized and strange political environment. Super PACs as roving extremist speech nuisances. Incredible that one man would redeem the entire idea single-handedly in 2016.

I made the filings with the Federal Election Commission, started to raise funds, and developed connections with a young consultant in DC who heard about us through our Twitter feed and was up for the game. But Ben's nature wouldn't allow him to settle on any idea for too long, and he was already up for the next venture.

"What are you saying?" I asked, trying to refocus.

"It doesn't matter if you've got the *best* weapons. And now the US itself can't end the positive *obsession*. It's like doctrine no longer matters. It's why I still admire Russia and the Chinese. They can't deliver the same technical precision, but they've built a system where they could fight you for a thousand years!"

"So, back to the gun-making idea you had," I said, ready to move on. Ben had brought up the idea earlier in the call.

"Well, it's surely easier now than ever to be an arms manufacturer," Ben began dutifully. I had expected it to be harder to change the subject.

Ben had helped introduce me to small arms, and his idea that we could make them for profit was one I would have only vaguely toyed with before. I certainly believed that free people were people with guns, but I hadn't ever before found the desire to be a part of the chain that placed them in their hands.

"But why bother?" I pressed him. "Any dude that's had a shop class and the right tools can do this."

I still ruminated on what our super PAC might have eventually meant. What had I even been playing at last year? By the time the summer had arrived, we had nothing to be proud of. Sure, we might have gotten lucky at some point in some race and made a little name for ourselves. But the best-case scenario was we'd have just pulled off a kind of prank, a joke. You can be snide and cynical about the electoral process, but that isn't truly a way of undermining it. Your participation, however ironic, is even a reinforcement of the values you hope to change. The system is surely ailing, and likely terminal, but is being a fly on that body worth much?

What was a better way to fight the world itself? To go beyond good and evil? What makes this sickened country leap to its feet?

"Say we do it digitally. Use a 3D printer. You've heard of those," Ben said, his tone measured.

I only barely recalled the concept. "Don't those machines only work with plastic? So, we'd make plastic guns? Is that possible?"

But as soon as I had said the words, I imagined an NBC anchor delivering the nightly news. "And now we turn to another story, seemingly out of the pages of science fiction. Three-dimensional printable guns, made at home."

Sure, make the guns with a printer, I thought. But if we could do it, anyone could. The political opportunity wasn't in manufacturing, then. It was in publishing. In one moment it solidified for me: we could produce a gun with the most widely available 3D printing technology and then freely distribute the plans over the Internet. We'd share the designs as open-source software. Go for the brass ring of system failure. Ben had given us WikiLeaks for guns.

"Defense Distributed," I said to him the next evening.

"Ha-ha, oh, yeah?"

"Yeah, that's what we'll call it. We'll do it with an organization."

"Defense Distributed," Ben said, as much to himself as to me. "I like the alliteration. I like what it suggests. It's a not-so-subtle negation, isn't it?"

If we were to proceed, Ben would have to continue to be my weapons guru. I hadn't grown up in a family that had firearms around, though once I reached a certain point in my life, owning a gun seemed like a prudent enough thing to do. Anyway, I had to trust his experience and familiarity with gun culture if we were to try to sell the project to the public. I was comfortable charting out the organization and the networking, finding the human and financial means to get it done. I didn't know a thing about engineering, ballistics, or plastics.

Before the call could end, I was already spinning out the rhetoric in my mind.

This is what access to the means of production was always going to look like.

Defense Technology? As opposed to what?

I did a little reading about the Maker Movement the day after hanging up with Ben. I had so quickly persuaded myself that besides American gun politics, ours would be a story of the history of the use of 3D printing. Running with an abstract and still undefined technology, we'd get to claim the highest ground of political realism.

I fed Ben new lines on our next call.

"Keep power in the hands of the common man. Make guns accessible. Forever."

I could picture him sitting in his apartment, game on pause, staring thoughtfully into the middle distance, already steps ahead of me.

"This could be really meaningful."

I cut him off.

"No, this could be a whole lot of fun."

————

By the time I had returned to Little Rock for the summer, Ben and I had taken to having walking conversations along the Two Rivers Park and its bridge. I invited my friend Daniel Bizzell along as a wingman to flank and needle Ben in the moments of distraction to which he was so prone. Along a walking trail in the darkened wood beside the water, Ben spun a strange parable about an arc welder. For a half hour Daniel and I were almost silent, absorbed by the telling as if it might arrive at some monstrous finality. It would not, but the trees cleared to reveal the river and the sparkling dam bridge across. Signaling Daniel, I suggested we sit on a bench just off the muddy bank.

"It's time for decisions," I said. "I want some calls about how this thing will be made."

"Did you hear about the palm pistol? Forty moving parts."

"We just need to copy a simple rimfire or a break-breech shotgun."

"Let the plastic do the work, keep the moving pieces to an absolute minimum."

"So, the Makarov—"

"Wait," I finally said, wanting to be sure we gained some traction. "We pick a round and design around it. Can we pick a round?"

Two hours of discussion and later, we committed to the .22. As it would turn out, we misunderstood its maximum chamber pressure, making our task even harder. Despite the misstep, simple blind choice had reduced some variables, and with that we could proceed.

———

Weeks later, when I returned to Austin, I spotted a cartoon cowgirl on a billboard. She too seemed transformed by the heat as she leered behind the haze that poured over the baked pastel city blocks. Once inside my townhouse, I brushed a spider's web off my arm and clicked the AC back on in the darkened hall. Left for months without air conditioning, my couch's fake leather had surrendered to a cloudy slick. The gremlins were about. The cable modem had failed and the local monopoly wouldn't repair it until the week following, so I'd have to find Internet in the city.

In ways literal and figurative, I couldn't afford to wait for the repair. With Wiki Weapon now pitched and advertised, and now that we'd established a loose organizational framework under my direction, we needed two things—information and money. That semester I was supposed to study the law of business organization, but I didn't think it would help me with DD. This wasn't going to be a traditional tech startup as far as I could tell. We weren't going to produce anything that people could buy, offer any equity, or have board seats to fill.

That was okay with all of us, but we were learning very quickly that there were no real blueprints to follow to get the project moving. And the results of my research into the history of plastic guns were growing more obscure, more mythic. Perhaps the Soviets had a plastic pistol in the seventies called the Troika, designed to slip past metal detectors. Defense research money for polymer weapons was real before the eighties. Then there was the Floridian gunsmith named Byron who had apparently stunned a roomful of Pentagon officials at an Army research center in 1987. His polymer gun was patented, but the document provided little meaningful detail. Each story's trail would abruptly go cold, its references quickly repeating. We figured we'd truly have to develop a design on our own. That would take more time, we assumed, though we wouldn't abandon the hope that we could copy some other plans and adapt them for printing.

After a summer of nights spent more often than not trolling the Internet imageboards for interest in the project, it was time to get more serious about fund-raising. Already, as I looked around my place, I pictured a pattern of expedition and privation. I was at UT on scholarship, but that didn't cover the rent, let alone the cost of the supplies and the printer we would eventually need. We'd estimated it would cost eighteen grand all told. I'd pick up any other expenses with my credit cards, if it came to that.

The year before, I'd learned a little about fund-raising from a young woman in DC who tried to help Ben and me while we attempted our super PAC. She told me people wouldn't give money away for an intangible reward that wouldn't be exclusive—even if they sympathized with you ideologically. And I was finding out she was right. It's hard to give people something for free.

The project would come at an additional price, though it was one that I was better able to afford. I chose to ignore my coursework—a decision I was happy to have the excuse to make.

By the time I returned to Austin in the fall of 2012 for my second year of law classes, I'd been in some kind of school for twenty of my twenty-four years. Eighty percent of my life. These were mostly pleasant years and experiences. No real complaints on my part. After making the decision to proceed with Wiki Weapon, I hoped I could still keep playing the role of respectable law student if I wanted, if the project quickly failed. The harder reality was this: if Wiki Weapon was going to be more than a game, I would likely have to devote my attention to it completely. In the immediate term, that meant raising thousands of dollars in the next two weeks.

To that point, we'd been successful in gaining attention but not so much at raising the cash. I had finished the website and added a PayPal donate button the very night before the first article came out. Even on the drive down to school at the end of the summer, I was scanning my email incessantly for donation notifications from PayPal. There was plenty of email. People had seen the site and found the Wiki Weapon project interesting, but the money just wasn't coming in.

———

The law school at the University of Texas was founded in 1883, and the building looks it. Viewing that part of the campus from the east off Dean Keeton, the tomb-white library rises from the hillside like a hardened knob. Inside, it's brown brick, brown concrete, and thin wooden paneling. In spite of an abundance of glass and light, the atrium and its adjoining halls remain dim and stale. In an odd corner the attempt is made to employ the drabness as a feature. A worn sweep hosts a painting of an old lettered man or a clutch of plaques. If you don't look too directly, you might sense the warmth of preftige; the frat house eminence. *And have you toured the portraits of the* politiques *before you*?

The first year of law school is called 1L and is marked by the blind groping of your peers. The anxious scrum, the nervous disease of it all, leaves no room for dignity. I'd often heard the story of some upperclassman making the Department of Justice honors program retold like a myth. And if righteous and diligent, we too might be swept up by that sweet, fiery chariot of Federal Selection.

There was a room on the second floor encased in glass where we could offer up our weird bodies for corporate husbandry. For what was our fulfillment but to become another object among objects? To allow our superiors to meet the challenge of choice? No, we weren't suffering a prostitution. We were pledging for Capital. As neophytes we might aspire to grind out our satisfaction at a hundred hours a week.

Pretending to myself I would attend classes for the new semester, I asked my buddies to write my name into our professors' seating charts. Without such help in Corporations, I walked into the room the first day and, as everyone rose to leave, blotted my name into a paper grid at the front.

Another week or two. I'd be back.

My fridge was empty. A temporary measure, I told myself, and at any rate it wasn't as if that privation would carry on into next week. I was more concerned with the state of the project's accounts. We'd only begun, but it seemed as if we were just days from going bust. If I could only raise a couple grand, I had no business stepping out of class. How much was my time even worth? I let everything go but courting potential patrons.

Sometimes I did radio interviews in the early morning, hoping to snag that first oil billionaire donor. On a grainy call on LRN.FM

(Liberty Radio Network), I told the host about my concerns. "Things are difficult since I got back to Austin and found my Internet wasn't working."

Ernest Hancock, who asked his listeners to *Declare Your Independence*, his effusive voice ringing out from a tower in the Arizona desert, found the humor in it all. "I bet! And you can bet that's *no coincidence*, boss!" During the breaks between segments he'd call me a slacktivist and I'd laugh.

By night I stalked the dark ribbon of North Lamar for corners in which to work. All quiet but for the isolate engine and the mutterings of a derelict rocking under the hard orange watch of a streetlight.

After hours I once worked surrounded by the modern, luminous interior of a McCafé. Perhaps the corporate architectural team—with a commitment to the environment, surely—had designed its spaces after the rooms in a home. In the café's conference area, framed in wood and aluminum, an old vagrant swore at CNN and tore at the waxy paper of a half-wrapped sandwich. A burnt-out half-wit beside him asked him to be quiet. I watched them fight as I installed a captcha plugin on our website. The half-wit cried for help from behind the counter, where the young, overweight women now only spoke Spanish. They slowly found something requiring their every attention in the back. In a booth directly behind me, a man's whispers to his partner became quick and aggressive. As he struck her and dumped his drink into her lap, she remained silent. The homeless men screamed at each other hoarsely as an ambulance idled in the parking lot outside, and I moved on up the road.

Three weeks into the new semester I sat typing under dusty lightbulbs in the shadow of Highway 183. This was Jim's Diner, and its Googie rooftop dipped as a quiet reminder of the Atomic

Age. At night the open blinds provided a view of its yellowed guests to passersby, not that anyone was looking. The younger waitresses would tell me about camgirling, their babies, and the trouble with dancing in Austin without a pimp. I would listen as I cut fresh email lists and bid out increasingly ridiculous Elance contracts, trying to find anyone with technical expertise. "Executive summary on ballistics instrumentation (under $500)." While there, I crammed for phone interviews about the project by reading obscure law review articles, pretending less and less it was somehow part of wandering back to my studies. I was living out of my laptop.

My inbox—*Why had I used my school email?*—was choked with dozens of false leads and promises of money.

> I may have what you're looking for. Call me. I want to share with you my work. I've solved most of this problem and believe I can help you. My partner and I would like to invest in your operation.

Wiki Weapon attracted a stable of soon-familiar suspects:

THE SOVEREIGN CITIZEN: Your main problem right now is that you are owned by the aristocrats, your title was freely given to the gov by YOU. We can fix this.

THE MYSTIC OF SPIRIT: Due to your catalytic tendency of disseminating objectives adverse to the Jurisdiction . . . of OUR LORD JESUS CHRIST, you are therefore ordered to discontinue your illegal profession. Failure to do so will result in proactive, responsive, and co-active measures.

THE CHASTE PROGRESSIVE: It is not too late to turn back, to return your donations, to renounce your lust for blood.

THE TOLERANT LIBERAL: I hope a hammer comes down on you . . . but I'd just as soon take the hammer of a gun pointed at your heart.

I toyed with them sparingly.

At Jim's I followed up on every lead.

Some were obviously problematic, but I pursued them anyway. An oilman had engaged me for over a week on the phone, his speech frequently broken. Each conversation took tragically compounded detours, and amid the noise I realized the sheer interminability of any process that might lead to a signed check. At his insistence I chased his offer to the slums of Houston, where I found a motel in as much disrepair as my host. He smoked synthetic weed, avoided my questions, and spoke haltingly of 3D printers in space. We watched my YouTube video promoting the Wiki Weapon while he mused aloud: "Six hundred thousand people have seen this. Do you get how many people that is?"

Six hundred thousand YouTube views and forty bucks could get you a tank of gas to Houston. Less than amused and feeling increasingly desperate, I later lingered with the man in a desolate, overlit Jack in the Box as he told me of his friends running drugs through the port, but soon nothing held my attention. Unwilling to spend another hour there, I took 290 back to Austin through the rising light of the early morning.

Shortly after midnight, two policemen entered Jim's and

scanned me. I cleared my head and responded to a reporter's email, agreeing to meet him on campus near the Tower. A new message. The striver teaching assistant in Corporations was supplementing my class assignments, of which I hadn't read a word.

Outside it began to rain. As I started to shake a bit from the coffee, I reminded myself to eat. While the cops were seated at a table to my left, I avoided their glances. My thoughts pulled me back to the summer in Little Rock where we'd begun, and when my doubt and suspicions weren't so pronounced. After wandering the streets of Austin alone for too many nights in a row, I felt I was embracing a psychological homelessness. When I looked for comfort or orientation, I'd reflect on those earlier months in Arkansas, wherein somehow I had found confidence.

In Little Rock I had decided to film a video pitch to announce Wiki Weapon with the help of Sean Kubin, the brother of one of my best friends from high school and easily the most infamous man from my hometown. The Kubin brothers, Sean and Zak, had the friendliest contempt for any kind of program. Their father was involved in advanced defense work before the turn of the century and would often leave them in Cabot with barely a word. "You boys have food? Well . . . all right." With time to themselves, they made quick mockeries of everything. Zak and I might undercut school fund-raisers, but Sean could change grades. I admired him most for kidnapping the local Arby's mascot and harassing the place with Polaroids and ransom notes. And still the brothers were kind and universally liked. I called Sean prepared to persuade, but he accepted my proposal purely from an eagerness for the mischief. He invited me to film after work at his Network Data Solutions office in North Little Rock.

Late on a Thursday near McCain Boulevard, I bought a DSLR at a Best Buy. As I left, the heat and the wind leapt off the parking lot's simmering blacktop to whip my face. I drove toward the molten horizon with a printed script. Sean greeted me when I arrived; with his close-cropped dark hair and heavy brows, he reminded me a little of my father. For only a moment I considered with respect the fact that he ran this little office by himself. With a firm handshake and smile he welcomed me inside.

"Great to see you," he said. "The room is over in the back here. Let me know if you were thinking you needed anything else."

By the time I was ushered to the storage closet to film, I knew it would be just me and the camera.

Abandoning the script immediately, I began, "Well, a group of friends and I have decided to band together under a collective name. We're not a company or a corporation . . . We just call ourselves . . . Defense Distributed. And we want to share with you an idea."

Sitting stiffly and avoiding the camera's cold black eye, I found ten tortured sentences to explain a Wiki Weapon. An idiot's testimony, which felt as enormous and impractical as giving the entire account of my life. I spent the rest of the night shooting and reshooting the same words in the same order. In the room over, Sean was laughing.

I checked in to the Peabody to finish the video, anxious that a final bit of ceremony might be enough to launch us. I spent the entire night listening to Kendrick Lamar and editing the distorted clips of myself on an old, cracked copy of After Effects. I uploaded the video to the first crowdfunding site I found that didn't have a prior approval process: Indiegogo.com. By the early morning the campaign was ready, and I slept until the afternoon, when I could drive back to Best Buy to return the camera.

Now campaigners, we began as any upstarts should—by declaring victory. Sean scraped together a list of all the national gun control groups from the web, most curated neatly for us by the NRA, and I prepared to fax-blast them a blank page with two simple words at its center: "IT'S OVER." "Printablegun.com," read the footnote. In an instant we pushed an Internet fax to every one of those empty closets and clapboard back rooms. To our delight, many of them failed. So many numbers disconnected. So many abandoned posts. Like playing Battleship for the gun lobby. Sounding with a spammer for an ultimate insight: If the enemy has folded up and shuffled off for mommy blogging, you don't take her off your website. That's bad fund-raising.

For twenty-two days I wrote pitch emails and letters. I watched the Indiegogo progress bar eke past one thousand dollars. At night I reread the crowdfunding site's terms of service.

"How much money have you got today?" my father would ask.

"Almost two thousand now."

He laughed with a shrug of disbelief.

Daniel Bizzell and I hosted late-night fund-raising threads on *4chan* in the cigar room at the Peabody. The waitress indulged us as we torrented gun manuals and engineering texts. As I pursued my at-home ballistics degree, I watched the project's YouTube video views tick upward every hour. The interest didn't translate to much Indiegogo money, however. And we were a long way from twenty thousand dollars. But I'd lately found ways to make my court at the old hotel more courtly.

My guest on one of those nights at the Peabody was Lauren, who, with her pale eyes, sandy-blond hair, and deliciously long legs, was much the object of my affections. We sat in the echoing lobby bar and spoke over a wandering saxophone, the player making long demonstrations of his circular breathing. Her lips were a glossy, muted pink, and she wore a tiny black dress that rode up her thigh. We'd known one another in college, but after our graduations it had been years since we were on the same continent. Even now, though she had always cultivated another demeanor, she let slip the loveliest microexpressions of innocence.

Lauren worked that summer for Arkansas's Heifer Project, an institute for mutualist agricultural lending sanctioned by all the right-minded subjects of progressive piety. She lived near the Little Rock Community Church in the old downtown historic district. Touring her neighborhood in a morning spent talking, we would pass the church and its pure-white Herod's Temple façade. Louisiana Street's own Holy of Holies, just around the corner from the governor's mansion. Lauren enjoyed mixed-income neighborhoods, new urbanism, community gardening, and meeting for lunch at the Clinton Library. In short, she was a beautiful planner, the kind NATO sends to Eastern Europe. I enjoyed her nonlethal aid tremendously.

We shared an intuition. Was it millennial? Some nights I'd join her house-sitting for bankers in West Little Rock. We raided their refrigerators like we would one day raid their 401ks—with the dim awareness that home ownership, country club dues, and large portraits of hateful little twins would never be ours. Sitting atop a high retaining wall on the riverbank, we watched the cool glow of the city and the blinking radio towers.

"I don't know. I'm beginning to think I won't be able to come back from this one," I confessed.

"The gun thing?"

"No matter how much fun you have, you're marked after trying something like this."

Lauren was driving me one afternoon in mid-August when I got a phone call. A New York number. The voice at the other end said, "This is Andy Greenberg of *Forbes*."

His voice struck me still.

"Yes," I stammered. "How are you, Andy?"

"So, I just have to ask. Is this real? Are you serious?"

I held my hand out to keep Lauren from slapping me, as she laughed with delight at the turn of events: her captive trying to give a serious interview. My thoughts broke and reassembled. "Uh, I see a kind of poetry there—sister technologies—the drone and the 3D printer. Just as you realize this totally operational state of surveillance, we pass the contraband underground, through the cables, as the drones fly overhead." I continued, gesturing expansively.

Lauren couldn't stand it.

We ended up at a bistro on the west side of town to celebrate. The story would run in the morning.

"You'll get enough money to actually do it, at that level of exposure," she said.

I yelped with glee. Before the check came, my phone lit up with an email notification.

From Indiegogo.

"I'll be one second," I said, walking outside to reread the

note. And just then I received a call, again from that New York number.

"Cody."

"Yeah, I saw it. I just got an email about it from their support team."

"What are they saying?"

I squeezed the phone screen, sapped of its depth in the setting sun.

"Someone flagged the campaign, man. I knew it was possible. I just figured we were past that now."

"Well, what are you going to do?"

I looked out over the parking lot.

"I'll figure something out."

I drove Lauren home then, as quiet as I'd been all summer. I wouldn't see her again until after the feds had shut me down.

The same night that Indiegogo pulled our fund-raiser, I put a Bitcoin address on the site and waited. Chilled, I watched the donations come in.

17.76
17.76
1.776
17.76
.1776

In the early hours I found an image of the Gonzales flag. I replaced the canon element with a RepRap printer and posted the thing to our website, proud to borrow the thoroughly Texan slogan, one suited for the skirmishes of all untimely men:

COME AND TAKE IT

More than a month later, I still felt some of that first bewilderment as I packed up my laptop. I dropped a few wilted dollars on the table and left Jim's for the damp night outside.

I had avoided other diners and cafés since my first weeks back in Austin. Everything to the south and east was choked with hipsters, sitting, malling, looming—mostly looming. But this far north they dared not gambol. No quarter for your bad conscience and mercenary affectations among the old and working poor, whose blind indifference was better than any contempt. Highway 1 led me slowly back to Guadalupe and home, where lustrous bands of white and green and red were pulled across the pavement's mirror surface. The night's work finished, I thought maybe I'd go to class tomorrow.

PART II

Ministry of Defense

One virtue is better than two, a poet once said. And like my plans to go to class, eventually most of my other virtues would be sacked in service of a strange new pastime.

At dawn the next morning I dressed slowly, deciding to continue my *other* education. I emptied my black nylon backpack of casebooks and crouched before a thin panel drawer beside my bed. From the cardstock boxes inside, I gathered a handful of brass and steel cartridges and two plastic shells, zipping them all into a pocket. Driving south, I headed for the law school but drove still further, ramping to the interstate and to coils of traffic locked in a bitter snarl.

Trapped in Austin's swollen arteries, I had nothing better to do than admire my fellow motorists' self-expression. The fashionable distillation of their interests and origins into abbreviations on white ellipses; 13.1 read one, halfway to my annihilation. I noticed the profusion of bumpers bearing the plain text, in white on blue, 2012. The upcoming presidential election, the grand deadline that had suspended not only this year in its political shadow, would be shortly upon us.

2012.

The next line to take in the trench warfare of our ethical progress: 2012—the emblem of our capitulation to the rudest historicism. The number was the message, a confirmation of the endless chain of electoral nonevents making up our eternity. If he dwelled on it long enough, a man could see why the innocent grasped at old glyphs in Mexico for evidence that Armageddon might finally overtake us; that in December the continents might mercifully drop into the sea or be consumed by the sun.

An hour past the jammed traffic, I turned off. Through a sheet-metal gate crested with razors, I drove between battered steel buildings in large white rows. I parked at the crumbling end of a dusty lot beside a shipping container and roadside-attraction sign with broken fairground lights. Its face marred by a crudely spray-painted DMT, the sign's peeling arrow pointed opposite a dumpster and to dubious bargains long forgotten. I walked, and then ducked under a half-open garage door and into a black wall of heat. When I made out the cannibalized auto bodies and metal entrails athwart the stained concrete, a young man crossed to receive me.

Moving toward him, I began, "My name's Cody. We emailed about 3D printing."

"Oh. Yeah! Hey, man, welcome to J&B. I'm Brent."

We shook hands. Despite his boyish face, Brent's battered work clothes and height left me unsure just how to place him. As he looked searchingly beyond me toward the back of the garage, I decided he couldn't be much my senior. A metal fan behind us only amplified the heat.

"Um, let's go get Jackson," he said. "Er, please, come sit down." He didn't seem used to receiving visits like this.

As I was led further into the shop, I saw that part of the space had been converted into makeshift offices. I sat in a rolling chair before a desk and watched through a pair of broken blinds as Brent found Jackson beside a stack of Pelican boxes. The two returned and I met the unshaven Jackson, who inexplicably, given the temperature, was wearing a canvas jacket. I shook his blackened hand.

"Wow, it's great to meet you, man," Jackson began. "We're excited about what you're doing. As soon as we saw the video, it was like watching the future."

"I told Jackson someone was going to try making one, " Brent added.

"Thank you. I know I'm not by any stretch qualified, but I wanted to make the case in libertarian terms—"

"What's it been like, man? The reception?" Jackson sat on the edge of the desk and squinted at me hard. His mouth hung slightly open, belying his obvious intelligence and enthusiasm.

I wiped my pants with my greased hand and settled my backpack beside the chair. "Well, I've got a lot of bitcoin. A lot of hate mail."

Jackson laughed. His eyes were bright and knowing. Perhaps he was capable of great cruelty.

"Yaa!" His voice rose in pitch and echoed through the back office of the converted warehouse space. "When I saw your video and you told those kleptocrats they didn't understand the world they were living in, I was like 'Fuck yeah, dude.' It's about breaking their hold on power, man. We get that."

"Thank you," I offered. "And thank you for your email."

"Like I said, we think what you're doing is important. But we're in business too, so, look, just don't name us in the press, and we can provide whatever you need—at cost. Here's what we're working with."

Jackson threw me a chain ring of little rounded keys, like pierced dominos. I looked over the clattering swatches, in shades of green and white, testing each in my fingers.

"That's PolyJet. Digital materials," Brent explained.

I had never heard the term. *Digital material.* My only reference was *programmable matter.* I wasn't too far off.

"Let's go see the printer." Brent gestured to me.

We walked into another area partitioned off from the main portion of the office. Beside a folding table and a yellowing monitor sat the machine, as large as an office-grade copier. With a forbidding density, it rose in large beveled panels of darkening tones of gray. Its massive printing head, abnormous and wired, sat behind a translucent blue enclosure—like some alien brain. Its chest bore the name Objet.

They told me it cost nearly a quarter-million dollars. The modeling material cartridges were seven hundred. And they handed me a green figurine all that money had allowed them to produce, which I turned over in my hand and pretended to admire. After some more talking we walked back to the desk.

"I'll have a printer in September," I told them. "I've done the application for a master trial with Stratasys. The material is ABS, like some of these." I held up the swatches. "I was thinking you could help me with design."

The boys smiled wickedly. Jackson showed me their pirated copy of SolidWorks, a software design suite for computer-aided design (CAD) and computer-aided engineering (CAE) tasks. I immediately liked that even a couple of generalist mechanics were digital pirates. A sign of the times, I supposed.

Jackson sat squinting at a screen, figuring his hourly rate for creative and design work. Brent stood, arms folded across his chest, his face blank. From my backpack pocket I pulled the cartridges. I named them, setting them on the desk while reciting aloud each caliber. The twelve-and twenty-four gauge, the .22, the .38, the .45 . . . I set them all on end like little tombstones. I had one last cartridge out but at the last moment thought better of it and thumbed it into a different pocket on the bag. The old Soviet 5.45. I'd forget about it until it showed up again as a holiday surprise for the Dallas TSA.

Counting done, I let them know what I wanted. "These are the common cartridges with the lowest max chamber pressures. Since we're working in plastic, I need to print something that simply survives an explosion. Think containment when you think about the failure mode. Even if it needs to look like some kind of geodesic grapefruit."

For another hour we drew sketches and compared figures on a whiteboard. I was glad that I'd done my ballistics homework the last few weeks, and that the boys knew the basics of designing parts for strength, but it was clear we were all lost as to our next real steps. I was okay with that, and even comforted. Figuring it all out would be part of the fun.

Soon distracted, we fell to talking and swearing like old friends. With patchwork beards and tiring eyes we made oaths and cursed our government.

That night, I got an email from a man named Amir.

Hi,

It might be a bit far for you, but I would love to have you
talking about the printable gun or distributed defense
(such a cool name).

http://bitcoin2012.com/speakers/

Think you could make London? :) I could try to hook
you up at a friend's house if you need a place to sleep.

....

Jesus pirated bread. Gave it to hundreds.

Baker: "We need better legislation."

I told him to give me a day to decide. And in a day I decided.

I googled him, Amir Taaki, and saw the name everywhere.
He even had a Wikipedia page. The Iranian-British hacker had
been described as both an enfant terrible and a key developer in
Bitcoin, the world's most exciting experiment in digital currency. From scanning the talk page on his Wiki, I decided our
views actually aligned. Taaki was hoping to do with currency
what I believed was possible with weapons—namely, to place
them outside state structures.

In photos, he gave off a monk-like affect with his dirty hood-
ies, his penetrating gaze, his almost-beard. He seemed to be ad-
vertising that he kept no share of what he had for himself. Like he
was always on his last dollar and enjoying it.

I read we were the same age, and I wondered for a few hours if
I shouldn't try to become a bit more like him if I wanted to be

seen as "influential." His fervent defense of open-source software as a kind of antistate politics was the first of a series of similar lessons for me, and so I decided it was worth the cost to travel to London. I'd be there to learn as much as to promote my project. I began reading whatever I could about the history and politics of free and open-source software.

The morning of the day I would leave for London, I first went to class. I must have been trying to bargain with myself, guilty with the knowledge I would soon be truant overseas. The day's lecture in Business Associations seemed interminable. Directly in front of me, a skinny blonde languidly browsed the *Corporette* blog on her laptop. For my part, I left up a full-screen *Drudge Report* to irradiate the poor bastards in the rows behind me. When class ended, we all milled out of double sets of doors, and I trotted to where I had parked to drive to the airport.

I smiled blandly as I took my freedom pat at security. A young mother ahead of me stood stooped and disheveled, her little children around her, as a slope-backed cretin tested her baby formula. This was a civilization worth protecting, after all. I hiked up my bags and passed a TSA sign that for years had been my favorite part of the Bergstrom Airport experience. In red, white, and blue: No Exit.

Standing in line, I noticed the posters on the jet bridge.

There's a new world emerging.
Be a part of the future.

HSBC wanted to tell me something.

HSBC.com/thefuture

I was sweating in the heat.

After connecting at JFK, I boarded for London. In the air I held close a copy of *Guerrilla Gunsmithing,* devouring the notes like precious secrets. Epoxies could add thousands of pounds of tensile strength to critical gun parts. Busted magazines could be strengthened with off-the-shelf coil springs.

Could you print a rifle magazine?

I flipped to the lovely author's note in the back: "Major politicians openly campaign on the promise to do away with our right to keep and bear arms. . . . Preserving our freedoms won't be easy. It's going to be a difficult, do-it-yourself project."

The guerrilla gunsmith reminded me of Philip Luty, a man from West Yorkshire, England, who made a point to publish his homemade firearms designs and host them on the Internet. He was imprisoned for years, chased to his grave with charges of conspiracy, incitement, and the aiding of terror. Download his books in the UK and as a special gift you'll have the Criminal Investigation Division serially raid your flat.

What I was trying wasn't new.

What to expect was plain.

I had only started the chapter on two-part glues when a pair of boomers across the aisle started talking about their careers selling life insurance. And how easy the smiles came. How happy they were to agree with each other. With a round of "I'll never forget," they launched into a salt-and-pepper conspiracy meant for every one of us surrounding them. Then the counting. Units, gallons, storage tanks, water softeners. Who knew they both enjoyed golf?

Recalled the taller: "That was the first place I ever broke seventy."

"I was out there with my CPA."

If in those days I had a natural enemy, it was the boomers. They infested the institutions. They daily erected monuments to their parents, that swindled generation gone down to death, and in laying them to rest had come to see their own bodies as prestige objects. They imagined for themselves a therapeutic state, every program of exemption from death, and impressed upon my fellows that it was all justice—that we should work so that they might be gathered up into the artifice of eternity.

Hours later I woke to a blue pulse. I traced it there in the darkness, some device's icy blinking, to a boomer's ear. The lords and ladies of Byzantium were close now.

"Reason for your visit?"

"I'm giving a speech."

"And you're here only for the weekend?"

With a slam I was stamped through Immigration. In those days the dour madams in military costume didn't send me to secondary. In those days Amir Taaki was still in London. I wondered what he might be like when I saw him at the conference.

The hour late, I found a car to take me into the city. I stopped between mansion blocks along the Embankment, under silhouettes and balustrades of marbled, sublunary splendor. I passed a bronze-plaqued corner and a crowd spilling from its polished step. A woman in fur, drink in hand, pulled at her friend with practiced ease. A man higher up the step, a cigarette thumbed to his mouth, eyed me without interest. I met his gaze and glanced at the open, richly upholstered room behind him. The laughter and loosened ties.

I took a room near the station, shortly finding my way there and to a grimed-up ATM. With a busker's bagpipe drowning out the call, I spent a few minutes pleading with a credit card representative. Afterward, cash in hand, I strayed down separate blocks as I made my way back, my eye caught by the moon reflected from the stacked rows of sash windows. Through wrought-iron gates I inspected the flats below the street and the fouling of centuries. Enormous figures of bronze and stone stood on pedestals at corners; down one avenue two leaned in repose above great columns. I was met with a sheer face of absolute concrete there in the dark. Ministry of Defence, read the plaque.

That night I saw a camera as large as a man.

I later woke in confusion. But instead of preparing remarks, I wandered about St. James. The sun broke between the rolling clouds, and I kept walking beside the iron street bollards in a hazy mix of hunger and sickness. Unwilling to address the jet lag, I used my time back in my hotel room to read about BitTorrent. About air rifles. About a CIA weapons shipment to the Free Syrian Army. The weapons' delivery was managed from a consulate in Libya, I read; it was attacked by Ansar al-Sharia. No matter, it was an election year. The important thing was that Bin Laden was dead and General Motors was alive. To suggest the same thing had happened to them both wasn't very progressive.

The Internet connection was fussy. Shadows stretched up the

room's embroidered curtains and across its walls and into corners. I ran a shower as I studied bickering fits between journalists on Twitter.

I flipped and scrolled through my inbox.

"Well, I'm confused," began an email. "Are you selling the items or plans or what?"

Abuse.

Abuse.

"I know how to make this a million-dollar business," concluded another.

In recent months I had been the student of an unhappy synthesis. It was as if the solicitation and the hate mail were in some way the same.

In a mirror I saw the steam turning under the light near the bathroom. It lightly danced to the coffered ceiling.

It's not even about the gun, I thought. What was at stake were flows of information: as long as these could be governed, enumerated, patented for sale or control, the state form and its thought were secure. Preserve the levies and hierarchies of official knowledge, and the universe is safe with just enough meaning. If that meaning included rat lines through Turkey or rip crews at Peak Canyon, then yes, this was a world happy to endure the hardships. We'd sing the *narcocorridos*, lyricize the bloody deeds of the corporate cartels, if their efforts delayed that ultimate and awful moment: not the conflagration, but the *flood*.

I left the underground at Russell Square with the afternoon crowds. No one told me to avoid the monumental stairway. After ten minutes' walking, I passed into the echoing internal courtyard of the Royal National Hotel, its rooftop just occluding the sun. Beside high glass panels, two men stood in dark hoods and glasses. The pops of heeled shoes and the murmuring traffic down the block swirled into the squared little space. The taller hooded figure shifted his simian bulk against a wall. He wore a light-blue surgical mask.

When I entered the first gray conference room, I took in the men and women seated and speaking. Behind a table I saw a dark young man directing a group of students. He was spry and his manner a bit bizarre. He spoke quickly and forcefully, with his hands gyrating and spastic, inviting the attention of those around him. His clothes were dirty and his hair a mess, but he directed his gaze with a complete alertness. He was enjoying himself.

"Amir?" I asked, louder than I intended, my voice rising over the buzz in the room.

"Ah, you're here!" he cried even louder than I had. Each party around us, now interrupted, briefly quit their conversations to watch our fussy embrace. He cheerfully pressed a patch of gummy, printed chain mail into my hand and looked on expectantly, that I might pronounce its worth.

"Ah! I want you to meet so many people. Let me go find Caleb, he's working on his own encrypted networking protocol!"

I sat awkwardly in a chair and watched Amir bound away. Hello, I must be going.

"Are you Cody Wilson?" a tall man asked. Beside him, a young woman was filming me. "It's wicked to meet you," he continued. "I've always thought that if I moved to America, I'd get a . . . well, what's that rifle? The tranq sniper rifle from *Metal Gear Solid*."

"The Mosin-Nagant?" I replied.

"Mosin. That's the one. It's perfect."

"Not kidding now, that was the third one I ever bought."

"Ah, so lucky. What's it like?"

As I began my quiet speech to the modest crowd, I offered that I represented the activist and the optimist. That our opposition only preached docility, authority, and futility. I leaned behind the podium, feeling a chill and a defensiveness. The ceiling panels overhead were unlit, and the air felt thin. I took up the 3D industry's popular analogy and added in some Eisenstein.

"Protestantism as an idea wasn't possible until there was the printing press."

It was a tool, I explained, which drove the complete inversion of the incumbent, Catholic order. What could we expect with self-replicating, networked, material printers? If man, irrevocably empowered and asserting his unalienable conscience, could dissolve his church, then whither his state? Was ending its domination a matter of mere historical condition? Would it just take a technical disintermediation after all—putting production into the hands of the individual?

"Will you have a gun? Will you not have a gun? No one else can decide for you anymore."

That was as comfortable with traditional political reason as I had ever been.

"As an Englishman I find this all abhorrent," said a man seated directly in front of me after the floor had been opened for questions. I stood in a line with three other speakers from the hours previous and began to address his Englishness as frankly as it was introduced. Amir leapt from the table on which he rested and in two steps had the mic from my hand, rocking from heel to heel in proclamation. I stood with my hands in my pockets, feeling the high black collar of my jacket against my neck. The room took to argument as Amir and I traded the microphone, fielding each inquiry and utterance with mounting enthusiasm. "I know this will sound crazy," a young woman eventually deadpanned from amid the rows of attendees, "but I have a question that's actually about Bitcoin."

The room broke into laughter.

Seated for a speech later in the day, I stared at Richard Stallman's shoeless feet. His misbuttoned shirt was taut across his gut. The paper program said he had invented the bulk of the operating system we know as Linux. From behind the podium he expounded on the virtues of compulsory education in free software while the anarchists grumbled in the back.

Amir whispered to me, "The woman you stood with earlier was Birgitta Jonsdottir, Icelandic parliament. She helped Assange put out the video—collateral murder."

"My God, I remember."

I was in a room with serious internet activists. I certainly didn't feel that I belonged in their company, but it was becoming clearer to me that the trip was well worth it. I had even picked up a piece of legal rhetoric: encapsulation. I meditated on it in silence, considering how best to one day use it.

The crowded room broke at the event's end, and I was steadily approached and encircled by the friendly and eager. A young Brazilian congratulated me.

"Do you realize the implications of your effort? What this means?"

I laughed and inspected my shoes, mumbling something agreeable. He spoke as if we'd already succeeded, as if the mere conception was the job done. I knew that a trial awaited me back in the States.

"I am surprised," the same young man said, his eyes narrowing and his lips pursing. "I think that you are more naïve than I had imagined!"

After briefly sitting with a journalist, I found Amir again. Together we teased a feminist student blogger on our way out into the open-air courtyard. She was mystified that anyone cultivated would direct such a heinous project as mine. For her pleasure, and to her visible dismay, I quoted Milton. "She knows that CAD files are dragon's teeth," I said, looking at Amir. "That being sown up and down, they may chance to spring up armed men."

He cooed with delight, slinking over and rising up to slap my back.

"Cody. A lot of people loved how you spoke. You'll come to the after party, yeah?"

I told him I couldn't.

"But you'll come back? I want to show you some of the work we're doing in Europe."

"Maybe we can collaborate soon," I said.

"Ah, yeah, cool."

I wasn't sure if either of us was being anything more than polite.

I walked back from the conference in the company of Haroon Khalid, a software developer I had hired early on to help with DD's website. I had sent him over to represent the project in advance of my presentation. Around the corner and far enough down the street, we turned and took the stairs into a yellow bistro. I asked him to order, my attempt to recover from the embarrassment of bringing pork to the table when we had briefly met the day before.

"How was the hackathon?" I asked.

He looked around the restaurant and then said, his face breaking into a huge grin, "Dude, DD was all anyone wanted to talk about. They had all heard of it."

"What did you get to work on with them? A mobile app?"

"Yeah, I'm thinking we can use a mobile app with, like, news updates and contest details. We can communicate with supporters and take in donors that way."

"Downloads?"

"I think that will work, yes."

I leaned back and twisted my mouth, watching his face, and then leaned in again. "So, listen to this. Say we release the gun, like the WikiLeaks insurance files, in an encrypted archive. A thousand, a million people download it, and like a Bond villain you tell the powers that be to back off or else you release the password."

Just then a waiter delivered a dressed-up hamburger with an absurdly swollen bun. The "American." Haroon sat wide-eyed, taking a quick glance up at the waiter in case he'd heard any of the treason just uttered. The day was fading and we finished the thought by candlelight.

An hour later, we walked back across a graveled parade ground and past low-walled checkpoints. The posted special police cradled knobby MP5s; the gunblack against their vests was deeper than the surrounding night.

On my plane home, an infant began to cry in the sleeping cabin. In a burst of light, the mother pacified her with an iPhone. In my seat I turned away from the child's pudgy, backlit manipulations, and switched off the television in the headrest at my face.

Before I slept, I began watching another screen a few rows down.

PART III

The Gun Printer

Soon after I returned from London, great boxes occupied my living room. I slid around and between them to reach my kitchen. In the early morning gray I sat amid the jumbled klotski, packed to the doors, and ate cereal in silence. In a few days I would turn the clustered delivery into a printer.

Later that morning, as I carried the pallets and straps behind the apartment complex, my neighbor said she had seen me with the deliveryman and the truck outside.

"What do you do?"

"I'm a gun printer," I said, my grin slightly slackening with distaste at the afterthought.

"How does that work?"

"Still trying to figure that out."

The boxes all read uPrint SE plus. I didn't open them at first. The packing slip and manual sat on my coffee table for a day, then two. When I stayed downstairs among them for too long, I began to feel a pressure at my temples. On the phone with Ben Denio, I could tell he was thrilled we had it. He tried to make plans to come down and see it. Maybe he could work with it while I went to class. I told him I felt too tired to even try to assemble it. It had taken weeks to convince a sales rep to accept the paperwork, and delivery had taken another week.

How to say it? For the moment I found the whole affair a burden.

"Well, we've got money in the bank, right?" Ben asked.

"Maybe fifteen thousand now. The printer people will want a few grand by next week."

"Well, calm down. What did you expect? You've got time now, so, take better care of yourself."

In the midday heat I walked down Guadalupe, past the university shops and the girls in their oversized T-shirts and neon shoes. Near campus, I took a phone call from a new number. A logistics company. I wasn't really listening.

"So, when can we pick up the printer?"

I crossed the street and, looking back, spotted a group of gutterpunks coming south and nearer. Shifting down the walk in blackened rags and rebozos, strapped into their packs all sun-bleached and dreadlocked and heavy with dust. Immortal destitutes, moving wholly apart.

"Hello?" The voice on the other end drew me back in.

"Look, I don't know what you're talking about. I just got it. Are you sure you mean to be calling me?"

"Cody Wilson?"

Roiled in the street, my face smearing sweat across the phone, I watched them pass. Like the living shades of the first—or last—

men to ever try this country. One walked in busted boots the color of spent coal. Our eyes met.

"You got a supervisor or something?" I asked, now frowning. "There's definitely a mistake."

"I'm just doing what I was told, sir."

"I only just got it," I said, still thinking this was all due to an accounting problem. One of those accidents you expect when you deal with any large, bureaucratic operation. "And I won't be giving it back yet, so, have someone else call me."

I stood idly as a bus clamored to the curb beside me to seethe and reek. I shook the conversation and picked up my search for the student clinic. The pain in my head was spreading.

Two days later, just after ten in the morning, my inbox held some official correspondence.

September 26, 2012

VIA ELECTRONIC MAIL AND OVERNIGHT MAIL

Mr. Cody Wilson

711 W. 32nd Street, Apt. 115

Austin Texas 78705

codywilson@utexas.edu

RE: Lease of uPrint SE

Dear Mr. Wilson:

I am legal counsel for Stratasys, Inc. We are aware that you have leased one of our 3D printers for a period of 3 months. We are also aware, from recent press articles and your blog, that you intend to manufacture plastic guns using our printer. We have received no indication that you hold a federal firearms manufacturer's license.

This email is to notify you that we are cancelling your lease on the machine and will arrange to pick up the printer and take such other action as is legally warranted.

We will expect to hear from you immediately by return email. If we do not hear from you within 24 hours, we will arrange for the immediate return of the printer.

Sincerely,

Claire Roper

Legal Counsel, Stratasys, Inc

Stratasys Inc. 7665 Commerce Way, Eden Prairie, MN 55344-2001
Main: 952.937.3000 Fax: 952.937.0070 www.stratasys.com

I was more interested in the "other action" Claire intended, but bristling, I shot back a response.

> Claire,
>
> Thank you for emailing me. I received a call some days ago basically asking me for the printer back without any other explanation.
>
> I must correct you, however. I will not be manufacturing firearms, as "manufacture" and "manufacturing" have quite specific definitions within the legal regime we're discussing. I will be making prototypes for personal study (not selling, distributing, or giving away what I produce), an activity that has never and will never require a federal firearms license. It is possible some of the prototypes will be considered AOWs for purposes of the National Firearms Act, but in this event the prototype need only be registered with the ATF and have its due making tax promptly paid.
>
> I'm afraid Stratasys has misunderstood either the nature of my effort or the laws governing firearms creation, but I trust it will respect the law of contracts.
>
> Crw

I may not have known anything about making a gun, but I could read the law all right. As an individual, you didn't need a license to make a gun in America. Not hard to find out. You don't expect a large corporation to change course after they send you explicit instructions, but I thought I'd let them know the law. Sure enough, Claire wasn't looking for a conversation.

September 26, 2012

 STRATASYS®

VIA ELECTRONIC MAIL AND OVERNIGHT MAIL

Mr. Cody Wilson

711 W. 32nd Street, Apt. 115

Austin Texas 78705

codywilson@utexas.edu

RE: Lease of uPrint SE

Dear Mr. Wilson;

I am in receipt of your email dated September 26, 2012 in which you state your opinion that your intended use of the Stratasys uPrint SE will not be in violation of federal firearms laws. You have also made it clear that you do not have a federal firearms manufacturers license. Based upon your lack of a license and your public statements regarding your intentions in using our printer, Stratasys disagrees with your opinion. However, we do not intend to engage in a legal debate with you.

It is the policy of Stratasys not to knowingly allow its printers to be used for illegal purposes. Therefore, please be advised that your lease of the Stratasys uPrint SE is cancelled at this time and Stratasys is making arrangements to pick up the printer. Please notify me when, in the next 48 hours, we can pick up the printer.

Sincerely,

Claire Roper
Legal Counsel, Stratasys, Inc.

cc. Thomas B. Heffelfinger

Claire,

I expected no other outcome. So, if you'll excuse the
poetry, come and take it.

crw

———————

In the morning, two boys jumped out of the cab of a mover's truck
outside my apartment. I didn't think I had time to tell Ben or anyone else what was happening. Sweating, they asked me if I had
some machine parts for them. A producer with *Vice*, who just happened to call at the time, was the first person I said anything to.
She asked me to film the printer being taken, so with my phone
raised I soon put questions to the boys about their task.

"Are you the logistics company?"

"Naw, we're local," one said, squinting as he walked past me
with the first of the boxes from my apartment. "They just hire us
out when they can't get their people on short notice."

The truck's engine filled the empty avenue with a low gargle. I
stood in the street filming like an aggrieved divorcé or land dispu-
tant. They carried the boxes quickly in the early sun. I was embarrassed at how neatly packaged it still was, how easy it all was to
remove. I took to tapping my phone, spewing emails, when they
had the trailer door down and threw the iron lock. When I could
no longer hear the truck's rumble down West Street, I called my
contact at *Wired* magazine. I couldn't think of another time I'd
heard of a similar repossession. Maybe the tech world would appreciate the story. Regardless, documenting DD's setbacks seemed
to be the only thing I was good at.

Claire cited potential illegal activity in her company's decision, but by now I knew the score. In the terms of my lease were Restrictions on Use.

> 1.4. Restrictions on Use. Customer agrees that it shall not directly or indirectly: (i) modify, enhance, adapt, translate, make improvements to, create derivative works based upon, disassemble, decompile, reverse engineer, reduce to any human or machine perceivable form, or circumvent any technological measure that controls access to or permits derivation of the source code of the Software or any part thereof; (ii) reverse engineer the Products, any part thereof, or any composition made using the Products; (iii) rent, lease, sell, transfer, assign, or sublicense the rights granted hereunder, except in connection with the rental, lease, sale or transfer of the entire System; (iv) copy any part of the Software except for one (1) complete copy thereof for archival and/or back-up purposes, or as otherwise expressly authorized by Stratasys in writing; (v) change, distort, or delete any patent, copyright or other proprietary notices which appear in writing on or in a Product (or in any copies of Software); (vi) make or permit use of any trademark, trade name, service mark or other commercial symbol of Stratasys without its prior written consent; (vii) operate or make use of the Products in any way violative of applicable laws and regulations; and/or (viii) take or permit any other action which could impair Stratasys' rights, or damage the image or reputation of quality inherent in the Products, Stratasys' business, reputation, Intellectual Property (defined below) or other valuable assets or rights. In the event Customer rents, leases, sells or otherwise transfers the Products to a third party, Customer agrees that it will require such third party to be bound by Sections 1.2 (Software and Documentation), 1.4 (Restric-

tions on Use), and 8 (Proprietary Rights) hereof as a condition of such rental, lease, sale or other transfer.

Buried in there was a clause stating that using the printer in any way that could damage the business's image was forbidden. I understood their position perfectly. Stratasys, Inc., wanted to avoid damage to their image. I was quoted in *Forbes* online telling anyone who would read that I was going to rent one of their machines. Why hazard the association with me if they could avoid it?

So, with few alternatives available, I decided I'd need to become unavoidable.

———

The next morning I drove to the local offices of the Bureau of Alcohol, Tobacco, and Firearms and Explosives (ATF), more from intuition than anger. What I wanted to know was simple: would I have been "violative of any applicable laws and regulations"?

I found a brick office building, identical to the others around it, and walked upstairs from an isolated lobby. From a corner on the second floor I walked into a gray closet with a shuttered, bulletproof teller window beside a heavy door. The fluorescent light faintly droned as I searched the cramped anteroom for signs of anything like human activity. I saw a single chair and an end table. I pressed a plastic button, which rang a bell, and listened.

"Yes?" Only a voice, through a speaker whose location I was unable to immediately determine. I hadn't thought of what to say.

"I just have some general questions I thought someone here might be able to help me with."

Silence.

"What kind of questions?" The voice came compressed, as through a cardboard tube.

"Well, I'm trying to do some ballistics research but it keeps getting suggested that I need a federal manufacturing license. I don't think that I do. Can I explain what I'm trying to do?"

A pause. The heavy door beside the window opened, and a slender Latino man looked me over.

"This is an enforcement office, sir. You may want to talk with industry operations."

"Well, where is that?"

"That's San Antonio."

"My questions are pretty general. Can I just run them by you and get your opinion?"

"Uh . . . as long as you know my opinion is not the law. What's your name, and I'll be right back."

"Cody Wilson." I didn't hesitate to respond.

"Okay, thank you, sir. Wait here." He gestured to the wall not four feet behind me.

I sat, looking at the threshold through which I had earlier come. Higher on the otherwise blank wall hung the seal of the Department of Justice and a framed portrait of the smiling president. There he was, the man who asked again only to represent our best, unrealized selves. But after the years, the portrait's glass is dusty, and the professional smile more disquieting. Of course, to abandon him now would be self-incrimination. *You* were the person you were waiting for, after all. I thought of that cartoon *O*, once the white sun rising on rows tilled red. Now it was the zero in 2012. That shift in meaning delighted me. Signs were brutally ambivalent, mocking even their most serious roles. Yesterday the sun, today the zero degree of politics. Tomorrow the wheel upon which our lashed Hope breaks to rattle in the sun. *Change was always a weak hypothesis,* some daemon whispers. *Things change; just like things stay the same.*

Wait, I thought to myself. This is an enforcement office? I shouldn't—

"What did you say your name was?" asked the grizzled man from the quickly opened door.

My mouth open, I managed, "Uh . . . Cody Wilson."

"Sir, I'm going to ask you to follow me this way."

I stood and pulled myself to follow the agent down a bare hall, slowing my gait. I jogged my mind for a handful of phone numbers, picturing the long detour through Justice the day might now take. The agent waved me to sit at a large conference table in an inner room. A tall, middle-aged white man came from a rear room adjoining and sat at the table's far end. My host sat opposite and nearer to me.

"We received a call about you."

I had had time to reserve my energy and admitted no surprise. After a thought, I broke the cardinal rule of all police interaction and spoke.

"I feel like this is an interrogation. Was the call about what I'm trying to do?"

My host began. His companion was writing on a ruled notepad. Suddenly I was every sap I'd ever read about. *Came right to them!* I listened while I tuned my voice to hapless academic. Their faces read confusion and restraint.

"The call was from a party concerned that you were illegally manu—"

"Stratasys? Stratasys called in a criminal complaint?"

My host glanced quickly to papers just under his forearm. *Now.*

"I don't believe it. I went through a months-long process with them and explained to the sales rep just what I was going to do. And this has been public news for months, by the way. Google me. I haven't tried to hide any part of my project."

"Well, can you explain what you were doing?"

"Have you guys heard of 3D printing?"

No sign of recognition broke over my host's face.

"I am trying to determine if it's possible to use one of these printers and its materials to build a ballistic chamber. Can extruded plastics be used to make a gun barrel? I came here for some legal clarity since everyone is giving me contradictory answers on whether this kind of *research* is in fact firearms *manufacturing*."

The writing stopped. The agents shared a humored, knowing look. *Intrepid little shit's just prepping for the science fair.*

In another five minutes I had talked my way back to the anteroom.

"You'll want to look over these too." The agent, grinning, slapped another fat paper book onto the pile in my arms. "State and local. Oh, hey. Here's the CD."

I backed out the doorway.

———

The running colors on Airport Avenue yielded to the yellows and reds of two-day body shops, lavanderias, and payday lenders. As I drove, an art board just over the razor wire of a tow yard peeked comically through the squalor. I tried to imagine myself as one of

those municipal committeemen, earnestly planning sensitive ways
to stem—or was it celebrate?—the city's visible rot.

"Those sons of bitches!" my father shouted over the line.

I had called him not just because he was my attorney.

"Yeah, man. Criminal complaint. It wasn't enough to just
take it back. They went for the throat for getting namechecked
in public."

"All that stuff is federal. They tried to ruin you."

"You know I'm hearing you. I only just stopped feeling the
pulse in my neck."

Light-headed after a few more minutes, I ended the call with
my father, glad that his response echoed my own. I needed a way
to digest this awkward brush with federal power, which I found
happening way too early. My father was always a sympathetic ear.
And it helped that we had the same temper.

I parked at a convenience store to return the last few hours
of emails and calls. The printer repossession story was on the
upcycle online. Word of it had spread to places like the *New York
Daily News*, CNET, and the firearm blogs.

In less than an hour a new call interrupted my handiwork—
from the ATF office I had left.

"Hey, man, it's Jones. We're getting a lot of calls here." He
sounded exasperated, his nasal sigh punctuating his sentences.

In the moment I felt vindictive. "Ah, yeah?"

"I'll tell you what I told them, you know. I just think Mr. Wilson is an intelligent young man. He's trying to do things legally—"

"I really appreciate that, man."

"People say ATF is antigun and all that, but I love guns. I support our rights. I'm a Cub Scout leader and I teach the boys in my

community how to shoot, you know? So, I'm asking, can you tell them, tell them they don't have to call here anymore?"

I assured him I understood these things and more. That I respected what he did, and that he was one of the good guys. I thanked him for helping me, but I had to go now because I was getting another call.

And I was.

Robert Beckhusen, my *Wired* contact, seemed sympathetic. He told me a hobbyist had pointed him to public promotions Stratasys had done with the big names in gun manufacturing.

"And do you know Abe Reichenthal?" Beckhusen asked me. "He's a CEO."

"Uh, the guy from 3D Systems?"

"Yes. He's got this open letter in a trade magazine from August where he calls on everyone in the industry to stop people from printing guns. Did you know about it?"

"I didn't, but it makes perfect sense," I said. "Look, I've been telling everyone since Indiegogo pulled us down that it was going to be this, quote, private sector that we'd have to overcome first. That Stratasys and these other guys act this way doesn't surprise me. It's this whole collusive, Family America thing. Industry as the engine of public policy. I mean, I literally just got back from the ATF, man. I know I'm doing this whole libertarian, federales-trying-to-reach-us thing, but at this point *only* the government has been willing to not cut my legs out."

I'd been freer with calling myself an anarchist lately, so I hoped an admission like that made me seem more reasonable to Robert. Libertarians have a habit of defending corporate decision making to better direct their scorn for the State. I just wanted to showcase the obvious bad faith that some PR team was trying to pawn off as "corporate responsibility."

"Yeah. Yeah, well, I think we'll run this. What are you going to do now? Am I on speaker?"

A pair of grown men had buzzed by me on miniature bicycles.

"Yeah, I'm giving this ATF guy's number to all these reporters. Gonna feel that heat."

We laughed. I replayed an image of Jones and the field office having to take or divert the calls, comforted that I might make them feel even a moment of the vulnerability I'd experienced with them.

"I mean, what did you find out? Will you get a license?"

"I still insist I don't need one, but that's beside the point now. I'm looking into it."

When I returned home, I pulled free a UPS mailer jammed into my doorway. I opened it and sighed as the sealed demands from Stratasys pattered to the countertop.

Thanks, Claire.

After *Wired* had the repossession story, every little wit with a blog had his pass. Not long read in the law, the technology, or guns, they didn't fail to quickly find opinions. I traced every backlink and screed. Every pseudo-profundity about fires in crowded theaters and corporo-social responsibility. The 3D printing world intersected with a group of self-identified "Makers," modern successors of the backpage DIY culture, who loaded online comment sections and forums with the liturgy of their movement, which as far as I could tell was mostly about the rediscovery of the personal use of tools and industrial equipment. They otherwise preached a kind of democratic celebration, but when it came to the printed gun idea, I saw only a patchwork apologetics for Stratasys. Some went so far as to say that the printer repossession was in fact the movement's will being done, that they had expected, even demanded Stratasys do it. The company best represented the Makers' interests and was protecting their progress. Looking for a better collision, I began to steer all my interviews to reach this camp, to appropriate their little fate phrases, and to dine on the heart of their "democratization." Who were these people? I wondered. Just what did any of them really believe?

"Worse than being mocked are the underlying accusations," I told Ben on the phone in early October, venting further about the online reactions. "Like I had no business to even try it! 'What are you doing not keeping your head down and working like the rest of us?'"

"That's really it, isn't it," Ben said. "Yeah, keeping your head down. Reminds me of another scofflaw, a guy fresh out of undergrad. He gets his degree in chemistry and immediately synthesizes MDMA. Doing a ten-year bit. Or, you know, there's this same suspicion anytime you call a chemical supplier as a private individual. It's completely inappropriate to be experimental in this political climate."

"I still think going public about our activities, our intent, is the only way we could have dared to get away with it," I said.

"But, you know, so many companies are building the infernal machine and just not admitting it. You remember the *Hellraiser* box, right?"

I grunted my acknowledgment.

"Ha-ha!" Ben cried. "But they market away from the maximal implications. Perhaps what was unpardonable in our case was simply not offering that fig leaf for our motives. We just admitted what we wanted to do. Solving the puzzle box in the open, playing with the forbidden so shamelessly."

In the first week of October 2012, when the story was freshly dead, I was contacted by the *New York Times*. The reporter spoke by phone with a curtness that I supposed communicated a journalistic rigor, an eminence, to which I was still unaccustomed. His name was Nick Bilton, and he asked me his list of questions with that breezy kind of disrespect we reserve for charlatans. Maybe he wasn't wrong. But in all the matter-of-factness I began to suspect he was taking pains to avoid my point of view in the matter.

It was as if, having found the story of obligatory reportage, he still begrudged it its merit enough to resort to the role of gate-keeper of record. Better to limit as much of this fringe thought from leaking into the account as possible. Yet he seemed to take a particular delight in a final question, a kind of wheedling mirth behind the words: "And say someone should kill you with your invention?"

When it was posted, the piece itself drove the points home well enough. The 3D printing machines will be capable of reproducing themselves. No place in the federal budget for an ATF agent in every home. Kids printing guns while their blissfully unaware parents think their young 'uns are playing on the computer. A prohibitionist is quoted as calling the Internet a permanent "gun show loophole."

And as expected, the article reproduced one of the more

provocative of my public statements. From the original Wiki Weapon video:

> What's great about the Wiki Weapon is it only needs to be lethal once. We will have the reality of a weapons system that can be printed out from your desk. Anywhere there is a computer, there is a weapon.

I was surprised that he described my voice as monotone. *Look out, folks, a psychopath.*

And then Bilton's article mentioned Michael Guslick.

> But this year, Mr. Guslick managed to print some components for an AR-15 semiautomatic assault rifle—the kind of gun used in the Aurora, Colo., shootings—on a 3-D printer. He used ABS plastic.

"The same plastic used to make Legos," Guslick had said.[1]

Now tell me the man wasn't a subversive.

I was overjoyed at Guslick's plain desire for mischief. He was throwing a big wink at everyone back home in flyover country.

I had heard and read about Michael Guslick for some months now. An amateur gunsmith and engineer whose efforts to make a partially printed AR pistol had made it all over the web. I found his approach to the media sly and entertaining. My favorite take on the response to the work of Mr. Guslick, who went by the on-line handle Have Blue, came from a blog by Scott Locklin:

> Everyone and his brother is reposting one of the many articles on the guy who used a 3-D printer to build an AR-15 lower receiver. They're making it seem like this is important, because pretty soon you will be able to use a rep-rap to print up an

---

[1] http://bits.blogs.nytimes.com/2012/10/07/with-a-3-d-printer-building-a-gun-at-home/?_r=0

AR-15. This isn't stats-jackassery, but it is the most pig-ignorant engineering jackassery I've seen in some time.

Ignorant, sure.

The Wired article isn't bad . . . but it leaves you with the impression that 3-D printed assault rifles are just around the corner. No, this is not possible. This will never be possible with 3-D printing technology; not now, not any permutation of it in the future. The guy who did this trick said as much himself; the media frenzy over this is ridiculous.

But that's where Scott and all the practitioners of scientism got it wrong. He dismissed without a thought the effect of Guslick's work as a symptom of technicity. Trapped in a pen of economic, working-class reason, he was angrily attached to a worldview of mere concrete production. He was unwilling to accept that he lived in a world operating just as much by a religious belief in technology, which has less and less to do with the facts of our tools every day.

What Guslick had done, in terms of concrete production, was to create a receiver, the piece of a rifle that houses its trigger group, grip, and magazine. And so what? Similar plastic rifle receivers had been commercially available for years.

Well, this receiver, sometimes called the body or the frame of the weapon, was, according to US law, the firearm itself. The AR receiver was the one part of that rifle that had its manufacture and transfer regulated by the government. As Guslick pointed out in the *Times* piece, you could go to your local gun shop and get any other component of the firearm with no questions asked. You could order the pieces over the Internet and all you'd need was a credit card.

So, what Guslick had done *metaphysically* . . . Well, he'd struck at the central value in this epoch of technicity: our sense of control. The Western world believed it had professionalized and institutionalized the production and dissemination of the firearm. It believed it had control not just over the acquisition of firearms but also over the future of the development of those firearms. I'd organized Defense Distributed to do nothing more than continue to attack that religious sense of security and control.

The first reader comment on Bilton's piece posted on the *Times* site was, judging by the avatar and the woeful invocation of Yeats, a boomer's:

> *Mere anarchy is loosed upon the world,*
> *The blood-dimmed tide is loosed, and everywhere*
> *The ceremony of innocence is drowned;*
> *The best lack all conviction, while the worst*
> *Are full of passionate intensity.*

I wanted to find him and talk to him. Did he regret that non-aggression pact with automation now? Eh?

Now the robots might actually *kill* the working man too? Where was his Oil Can Eddie when he needed him? But then who can deny technology and its progress? Reinforced by this enormously positive, indisputable monopoly of appearances, this dogma subsumed all others.

And "Now the Guns Will Be Printed," says the *Times*. What amazed me more than anything else was that each species of bitter response to the article could still only amount to a deafened acceptance. They were helpless. The news was as useful to them as if they'd discovered the divine perversions of the Great Overseer.

Maybe Wiki Weapon really was the Second Coming.

Regardless, it was the future as written by the *New York Times*, and every sensitive liberal knew not to argue with that.

———————

A day or so after the *Times* piece ran, a man named Daniel Fisher asked to meet me. He said only that he wanted to help, and told me he was starting a firearms business. I would find him at a deli near campus on a Saturday morning. Outside the place's door I stood leaning over my bike for a quarter hour. Across the square and overhead, the girls sat sunning themselves on the quiet patio of a coffee shop. A tall man walked toward me. Without ever having seen him before, I knew him by his shirt: "Zombies don't care how you voted."

Daniel was tall and blond, of a solid build and wearing those wraparound shades that always seem to uncomfortably divide a face. His voice was frank and colorful. And if he intimidated, it was only by his lengthy knowledge of weapons systems and his obvious experience as a machinist. We ordered at the counter and found a round table in a corner near a window. He told me of the times he'd attended the SHOT Show in Las Vegas, and about his activity on the AR-15 forums. I nodded along silently in total unfamiliarity. He listened to Joe Rogan and Alex Jones. And there I found a foothold.

Alex Jones had a huge operation in Austin. He was an independent media baron with the talent and charisma to sell every event and act of God as the positive signal of a coordinated, protean plan for the New World Order. He preached a government of the sheeple, by the sheeple, and for the sheeple and was the biggest thing on the radio out here.

His news program was called *Infowars*, and it attracted the preppers, truthers, birthers, and the soldiers who had returned from abroad to realize they might just have taken up arms for people who hated them to the bone. It was the veteran I thought of the most. The simple elemental of the war machine, unsure why it was now his lot to wander at the margins, to hold a cardboard sign at weathered intersections.

Jones's greatest work at the time was a documentary called *The Obama Deception: The Mask Comes Off*. The thesis was that all the idolatry and marketing from 2008 was orchestrated by the secret cabals of power. That it meant a hidden domination.

And I understood why positions like Jones's were necessary: they provide us with the vital illusions we can hold up to shield ourselves from deadlier thoughts. That there might be a hidden power behind the throne provides an odd comfort, when you think about it. It lends itself to a sort of negative religion. Even if the story was tragic, at least there was a plot. Even if it was Moloch's, at least there was a plan.

Only don't tell me that every form of servitude is voluntary. Don't tell me that the curtain hides nothing. How do you make a DVD about that?

I asked Daniel casually, "You're into *Infowars*, then?"

He nodded.

"Yeah? Well, they're coming over later to my place to film for the nightly news."

Daniel smiled, chewing his sandwich and nodding, as he

leaned over his elbows at the table. In the early afternoon light he seemed resonant with unspeakable calm and stability. A fullness that I couldn't know, even if he had offered to explain it. He asked me what Jones was like, but I couldn't say. I had only dealt with a reporter who seemed to be a kid just like me.

After more chatting, Daniel made his purpose known.

"I live in Fredericksburg. It's west of here a ways, north of San Antonio. Close to Boerne, if you've heard of it."

"Boerne." I paused and sent my eyes searching the place as if I could see a map. "There's a CIA weapons depot there, right?"

I hoped he'd like that. Sure enough, he gave an approving look.

"My brother and I are probably getting an FFL soon. I've been studying it for a while. Saving up the money. And you know, I saw what happened to you guys and I just wanted to offer you the use of our space and the license if you want to keep going. If you need an FFL to print the gun."

I was thankful. A federal firearms license would probably be enough cover to get us to the finish line. Every node in the white market seemed to want to see your state credentials to do this kind of work.

"I've been looking it over," I told Daniel, not going into any detail about my trip to the ATF offices. "Getting one myself, I mean. Maybe you can tell me about it? How long it takes and all that? Could I do some work off-site and bring it out to you for registration or what?"

"Well, the FFL and any FFL activity is tied to a licensed location. And the place has to be zoned for at least light industrial." Daniel rubbed his chin and went on, "Where do you live? I don't know, but I'll bet you your place isn't zoned for it. Austin is kind of famous for zoning out gun work. But I'm so far out we don't really have to worry about it. In fact I checked, and I'm not even zoned *at all*."

I said I was interested.

"Just come on out if you want to see the place. I'll take you out to Alamo Springs. You can meet my brother; he's pretty good with industrial design."

I promised him I would.

A new week began, and I drove back to J&B. As I swung open the metal door beside the closed garage, I stopped, impressed by an old BMW engine block that sat haphazardly beneath a steel rack. Through an office doorway I saw Jackson and Brent standing close and loosing tense whispers. I walked to them, and Jackson said he'd be a moment. Brent led me to the rear office and, while polite, was not inclined to speak.

I was opening my backpack when I glimpsed Jackson now arguing with a woman toward the front. She was holding a green, printed lamp.

"I've been reading about you, man. I think DD is going to blow up."

I looked up at Brent, who now appeared younger than me in his bulky coat.

"If you need a project manager or something, I'd love to be considered."

Jackson walked through the door beside the printer. I spoke, nodding to the window beside us, which only offered a view of the back half of the shop.

"So, what are you guys doing with all of those Pelican boxes?"

Brent started to speak but squinted and thought better of it. Jackson ran his tongue across his lips before he began.

"Filling them with guns and MREs, man. Bugout stuff."

"So, what, you guys are heading out soon? That looks like a lot."

They paused.

"You know the score, man. But don't tell anybody about what you've seen." Brent's demeanor and the more important mission I'd come on suggested that it was time to drop the subject.

We passed out of the offices and onto the rubber mats that lined the back of the shop floor. I looked to my left and took in Jackson's Jeep, the stacked wooden doorframes, and a giant pile of broken particleboard.

"So, I'm guessing you guys saw what happened to my printer."

"Pretty hilarious, dude," Jackson said, shaking his head and raising his eyebrows.

"What are you thinking now?" Brent asked.

I clapped my hands together. "I print with you guys while I wait for a license. Maybe I could even tie my license to this location? Eventually."

Jackson was now chewing on some kind of energy bar. "Like I said, I'm ready." His response was muffled by the resinous effluvium in his mouth.

"There are still some things we can do first. There's this guy named Guslick, and his AR-15 lower receiver is over at Thingi-verse. The big online repository. It's never been on video. So, we'll start with that. Duty demands we make a working rifle with it and fire it in HD."

"Okay, let's do it." Jackson pumped his fist and stepped back like he'd just broken the huddle. "You've got the file?"

"I can show you where it is online. But wait, how much to print?"

Jackson rolled his eyes. "You know, it's always the same thing with everybody. I'm sick of this hurry-up-and-wait bullshit."

I held up my hand, sidestepping whatever bizarre fight he must have wanted.

"Look, I'll come back with the file and the cash and we can go from there. Just get me an estimate."

Matte black with a brilliant vented dome, my father's old desk lamp was the only light on in the apartment as I worked. Though I rarely glanced at them anymore, I found encoded in the vent's points of light all the silent profundity of childhood remem-bered. The glow was sufficient company in the silence. That and open lines on *Coast to Coast AM*, the radio haven for fringe sci-ence and conspiracy theories, where you could hear your fellow man's brain break at thirty-four past the hour across America. All brought to you by the Ad Council, and the foundation for a better life at values.com.

I sat half-naked in my office chair, and into the early hours worked through stacks of state and federal forms. Proud and em-bittered, by then I had started calling DD a hydra. Behold a money company, a gun manufacturer, a publishing corporation. Not only would Defense Distributed do it, not only was there no possible legal or political mechanism to prevent or deter it, but I could find in this slurry of codes and federal regulations a way to make gun printing tax-exempt. We were educational, scientific; we even lessened the burden of some obscure government obligation. An antihumanist charity. I printed triplicates of certifications and copied my penned signature. Not only would the event happen, I'd get it subsidized.

"Remember when I said it was a million dollar idea?" I texted Ben. "It meant we'd have to spend a million."

While I was in the middle of finishing a final form, Haroon sent me a link to a video of Andy Greenberg speaking at a National Journal Government Executive conference. The reporter was explaining the motivations of his recent book:

> But I wanted to trace the ideas of WikiLeaks back to their roots, and I found them in the cypherpunks, this group of guys in the early to mid-nineties, ultra-libertarians mostly, who saw the ability to use encryption, use secrecy and anonymity technologies to take power away from the government and give it to individuals. This kind of began with a guy named Phil Zimmerman, who created PGP, a software I'm sure everybody here has heard of, which was the first freely available encryption tool that was uncrackable, even by the government.

> And this did scare the government. I mean as we heard about earlier, Phil Zimmerman was investigated for exporting PGP as if it were a munition, as if it were a bomb or a missile. And I think really this was the first example of the *Streisand effect*.

> I don't know if you guys have heard of this, but Barbra Streisand in 2003 found a photo of her Malibu beach house online.

> Never mind the fact that it was actually just one photo of it in a collection of hundreds taken by this environmentalist who was photographing the entire California coastline. She saw this photo and sent him a cease and desist. And the result was that we've all now seen this . . .

Andy was pointing to the picture of Streisand's house.

> . . . which she helpfully identified for us. Nobody knew which of these photographs contained her house until she sent this note from her lawyer. And now this is a meme. It was picked up by the AP; it was spread all over the world. And Barbra Streisand got her name put on this—effectively what happens when you try to censor something and instead cause a backlash that makes it proliferate everywhere. Something similar happened with PGP, and the government's attempts to suppress it. This really excited the cypherpunks.

The cypherpunks? I made a note to look into all that.

On another night spent plowing through paperwork, I found an email from a self-identified Maker accusing me of "Open Source Terrorism." The Maker Movement's ethic of access, openness, and inclusivity still didn't mean you could ruin it for everybody. I liked his reasoning. I saw it a lot.

Obviously democratization is too important a task to let just *anyone* do it.

He was completely serious, of course. Most of them were. The more banal your position, the more sacrosanct it's allowed to become.

But what to make of these Makers? You could say they were almost radically apolitical, and yet there was this spiritual complicity with power—a need to have legitimized their new Industrial Revolution. This pop talk about "access" was like that of "tolerance." Everyone had the right to an uninterrupted voyage to a fabricated future free of all negativity.

Maybe I still wasn't taking my work seriously enough. I set myself to digesting the Maker Movement manifestos, some literally so titled, but each seemed to read more like an advertisement or the marketing paper for some startup. One of these thin pieces of cheerleading almost had to be paid for by TechShop, which as far as I could tell was a new kind of gym. Come one, come all, to hack, craft, tinker. I'm sure there was a startup struggling for even softer euphemisms than these.

The Maker battle cry: "To make stuff! Together!" Press a Maker enough and he says he wants to change the world. But a tinkerer's manifesto manifests a tinkerer. His is no Luciferian revolt. And who was to lead his "Next Industrial Revolution"? He might tell you Bre Pettis of MakerBot Industries, whose first product was named the Cupcake CNC.

Yeah, these revolutionaries were out for blood.

Playing for keeps.

I got no further when I considered the phenomenon that is Maker Faire. Perhaps that was the better object of study. On makerfaire.com's homepage, they revealed nearly everything I needed to know:

Maker Faire is the Greatest Show (and Tell) on Earth—a family-friendly festival of invention, creativity and resource-

> fulness, and a celebration of the Maker movement. Part sci-
> ence fair, part county fair, and part something entirely new,
> Maker Faire is an all-ages gathering of tech enthusiasts,
> crafters, educators, tinkerers, hobbyists, engineers, science
> clubs, authors, artists, students, and commercial exhibitors.
> All of these "makers" come to Maker Faire to show what they
> have made and to share what they have learned.

This insistence on the lightness and whimsy of farce. The romantic fetish and nostalgia, to see your work as instantly lived
memorabilia. The event was modeled on Renaissance performance. This was a crowd of actors playing historical figures. A living charade meant to dislocate and obscure their moment with
adolescent novelty. The neckbeard demiurge sees himself keeling
in the throes of assembly. In walks the problem of the political
and he hisses like the mathematician at Syracuse: "Just don't mo-
lest my baubles!"

It wasn't just the Makers who were bringing me down. "But
you could have printed anything!" the reporters would announce
when they met me or found me on the phone. Like it was the first
time I'd ever heard that. Like it wasn't as readymade as the hot
plastic iPhone cases falling out of the printers they filmed.

The popular 3D story that week was a toddler with a printed
back brace. The cherub in her armature would even make *Good
Morning America*. I recall my friend Bizzell had asked a buddy
around this time, an obese Maker, to visit him in Fayetteville and
bring his printer. A Solidoodle, or one of the other boxes with an
equally noxious cartoon name. But the Maker could only fit his
keg in the car; they'd have to print another time.

And why not? *Today I brought the keg, tomorrow I'll bring the printer*. The perfect confirmation of the general economy of equiv-alent social identifiers into which these magic boxes slipped. Were made to slip. Just id machines, producing ourselves to ourselves.

You could have printed anything. Something helpful: a prosthetic.

Why didn't you print a prosthetic?

The goddamned printer was the prosthetic.

PART IV

Terror

I told them their fathers had rebelled for less. I tried to make eye contact with as many of the nearly two dozen students crammed into the classroom as possible. The November air in the third floor of the College of Natural Sciences building was musty. Jose Niño, the president of the Longhorn Libertarians, had invited me to speak on campus. I looked at it as a chance to hone some rhetoric before a friendly crowd. In situations like these, a guest isn't supposed to go on the offensive. But I figured, if nothing else, I was going to enjoy myself.

Our topic was "Emancipatory Terror."

Why did they feel like they needed so much more cover? I asked my brothers and sisters, What held them back? Was it "legitimacy," the unripeness of the moment, or was it simply fear of violating the law?

I spoke as fast as I could, looking past them now and again. The words were increasingly for my own instruction.

The speech became a homily on progress. Why were we, brothers—if you are indeed my brothers—so comfortable as the defeated subjects of other men's ideals? You say you have no gods, but there you stand immobile in the gaze of some Big Other— some outside point of reference used all the same to judge the final meaning of your actions. As if at the End there will be a report.

The students tittered and looked at me with sure smiles. But I saw the growing discomfort and fascination. The fast-breeding insult.

I told them about one of the national gun control groups naming me an "American insurrectionist." A group funded by the Methodist church. And was it any surprise that the Methodists, their church not so far from their state, ran a virulent gun control operation?

I liked to picture them as wobbling ecstatics, still at the benches in the DC Methodist Building, shuddering in fits after the *Heller* decision came down. They'd find yet another way to experience the *eschaton*. Theirs was the perverse enjoyment of feeling they'd survived beyond the end of the world.

With one of their surrogate groups they had assembled a running journal of events to document America's insurrectionist tribulation in preparation for the Millennium. A catalogue made for handing over at the Judgment seat, for the coming Prince.

These prohibitionists were nihilists too. I disliked not only their need to purify themselves from contact with evil, but the idea they had to clean up history as well. They whitewashed two centuries of thought on the universal militia as mere reaction propagated by the "fear industry" at the NRA.

Not that it mattered any longer, but the kind of fevered republicanism that gripped England in the early 1600s yielded rare political fruit. Figures like James Harrington and John Toland had refined a species of moral economics and politics that would deeply affect the American founding over a century later. They were elaborating their ideas in a world transitioning from rule by divine right of kings toward self-government. Could they reinvent the republics of the ancients? Much of their task was to develop a new civic humanism capable of shielding their republic from an inevitable corruption.

One of the terrifying and outstanding concepts the Harrington republicans developed was the universal militia. Instead of a ruler hiring a mercenary army or establishing a standing army that owed fidelity only to the crown, every freeholder would be responsible for providing for the common defense and practicing with arms. The republican radical believed not only that this kind of responsibility would cultivate a better citizen, but that a nation with a universal militia would be less prone to throwing itself into unnecessary and foreign wars. The commonwealth might be kept in a more defensive posture, and the people better able to tend to their own affairs. Though now this seems an unlikely thought, it seemed a prudential model to the radicals of its day. The universal militia might keep the common citizen freer in the long run while dislocating the corrupting influence of power from a single sovereign or gang of oligarchs.

Thomas Paine and the urban radicals of the American Revolution were familiar with the so-called standing army controversy as well, and the ideal of the universal militia was carried right over to the foundation of American gun politics. I told my audience I believed the Second Amendment to be a vestige of this now entirely foreign, paradoxical republican debate. A concrete legal protection of a citizen's right to violently abolish the law. A miraculous rarity in history.

A concept so unique that we may never see it as a part of state-craft again.

To the American prohibitionist, ours is too inconvenient a political history.

I looked down to my notes, speaking to the students again. In private I called the prohibitionist denial, its eliminative move, the Gatsby strategy.

"It wasn't enough that the prohibitionists have the concrete power to take your guns away, to divest you of them. It's important you recognize the guns were *never* rightly yours to begin with," I told the assembled.

History itself, like every sovereign thesis, was a threat. Threats have to be eliminated.

This whitewashing, recriminative view of history, this fumbling exegesis, was part of a syndrome of repentance. We had read the bedtime story. It was time for the fulfillment of a global democratic epoch of nonpolitics. The modern academic and state machineries, the abstract engines of human domestication and subjectification, were all aligned in service to the principle of a Bare Life Movement. *Every political question has been answered*, says the modern state. *Go to sleep. Destiny is unavailable to you.*

"Revolutionary" thought (is that the right word?) would require a passion for a real and virtuous terror. If you dare to chart a divergent course, you should also muster the awful might to initiate it. You can't just envision it; you have to implement it.

What separated Defense Distributed from the impotent was

that when we said "universal access to arms," those who listened understood we *meant just that*.

Universal access to arms.

We not only meant it; we intended to take the fanatical steps to enact it. Say the *New York Times* asked in malice if you feared death by your own Wiki Weapon. You revealed a mad authority, a full-figured sovereignty, if in response you simply sniffed. Who then was the first gun printer? If the herd cried *Prometheus*, I heard only *Titan!*

I concluded the presentation by reading from the works of Tim May, whose essay I had found with others in an anthology in the main library on campus. May had a profound impact on a lot of digital radicals' thinking in the nineties, and now, I supposed, on my own. It seemed appropriate to end with a few lines from back in the relative dark ages of 1992 in May's *Crypto Anarchist Manifesto*:

> Just as the technology of printing altered and reduced the power of medieval guilds and the social power structure, so too will cryptologic methods fundamentally alter the nature of corporations and of government interference in economic transactions. Combined with emerging information markets, crypto anarchy will create a liquid market for any and all material which can be put into words and pictures. And just as a seemingly minor invention like barbed wire made possible the fencing-off of vast ranches and farms, thus altering forever the concepts of land and property rights in the frontier West, so too will the seemingly minor discovery out of an arcane branch of mathematics come to be the wire clippers which dismantle the barbed wire around intellectual property.
>
> Arise, you have nothing to lose but your barbed wire fences!

As the crowd dispersed in a murmuring tumult, Jose Niño approached to thank me for my time. I thanked him in turn for giving me the opportunity to practice my craft. He was followed by a writer and a photographer from the school paper. I saw others lingering in pairs around the desks in the back. Over the next few weeks I would meet most of the people who attended, each of them stranger, more difficult characters than I had imagined. But each offered to help in whatever way they could to breathe life into Defense Distributed.

I walked out of the building that night with a sense of accomplishment that I hadn't experienced for a while, a different kind of satisfaction. Though I was surely preaching to the choir, from those hours of preparation to the presentation, I was able to finally put into words my most recent fascinations. It was startling to read just where I had allowed my thinking to travel in so short a time. Prepping for the interviews on TV or the radio was really just a game. You're competing with a producer to pack something unexpectedly "red pill" into an unavoidable sound bite. That's the best you can hope for, anyway. So, all my recent reading had had no real outlet. I was amused that I had let loose so forcefully on the students.

Ben and Sean from back home were still checking in to pepper me with research and development ideas. Funds were trickling in with each little article online. I was still emailing in the dark to find donors. But if we were going to make real the looming threat of a downloadable weapon, we'd have to create a proof of concept.

And I was still nowhere closer to getting there.

We'd already claimed the political many times over in the media.

Enough of that.

I had another worry I wouldn't admit to myself at the time as well.

I worried that if this took a few months longer, I wouldn't recognize myself.

The night of my presentation I went downtown to meet a small man in dress slacks and a flat cap who after the speech had introduced himself to me as John Henry Liberty. He had stood too near me, and we'd begun a little dance as I backed away and he advanced. Despite the comedy of our introduction, I agreed to meet him. He told me he was a programmer.

Near ten I hit a parking deck on Seventh and walked to the piano bar of an Old West palatial. At the side street was Mr. Liberty. Together we took the hotel's side entrance and, after climbing the stairs that edged the extravagant lobby, found a table in a darkened corner. The place was lush with music and conversation. My eyes skipped over the low, pressed-tin ceilings. John Henry Liberty took pains to detail his ethics, his run for office, now recently failed, and the trust fund kid who had sponsored him in the endeavor. He spoke of software ventures and of a sandwich in some local shop that bore his name.

As he did this, I studied a silent sculpture under a dome of green-stained glass in the middle of the bar. Two bronze horsemen are locked in unheard struggle atop an enormous rock. The leader's foot is snagged in the stirrup and he is dragged on his back, frozen in a moment of peril. His companion strains with a rifle in mad pursuit but will never, never shoot the runaway.

I interrupted Mr. Liberty. "Right now I'm doing this thing where I ask the public to submit gun designs for testing. So, it's like outsourcing the work. I was thinking this could be a model for collecting designs in the future anyway, but I'm sure submitting the files is not without some perceived risk on the part of the donor."

"Okay, go on."

"Well, are you familiar with Tor?" I asked. "Onion routing—this system to allow anonymous Internet communication?"

"Definitely."

"I was thinking about using a Tor-hidden service at an alternate web address. People could go to a deep-web dropbox if they wanted to leave DD designs—or download them for that matter. You see where I'm going?"

"Definitely. Definitely."

He bounced his right leg as he spoke.

We kept on for some time thereafter. I detailed the process I wanted, checking now and then to see if he followed. If he might be able to write the code. Always yes and yes. Not a problem and not to worry. When the bar was emptied and the cowhide seats sat fat and exposed, he gave me his word. He'd get it going tonight and report back in the morning.

Of course I never saw him again.

———

Jose insisted he had enjoyed the speech and emailed me a few times in the week after. He wanted to connect me with members of the Austin "Liberty scene," and I believed that meant their money. I was introduced to plenty of names by email. Members of an old guard that I probably should have recognized or respected. Jose invited me to meet him at his work. Apparently I had to see it for myself.

North of the intersection of MLK and Guadalupe, just south of the weathered Catholic mission and the crowded bus stop, sits a Chase Bank entrance in plastered concrete. You might look south from there for the capitol only to see a huge billboard for boots. Instead of walking through the row of doors to the bank, you take a left and pass a corner newsstand before descending a long staircase. At the bottom of this passage is Brave New Books.

Just before turning through the shop's glass-pane threshold, I stood agog before a cinder-block wall festooned with every species of flyer and circular. Fresh pamphlets were pinned over discolored meeting announcements, which themselves papered over aged printouts decrying everything from fiat currency to the murderous Austin police department. Higher up the wall and pressed over a large swath of this paper scaling, I saw a large cardboard poster of the president, arms folded, framed in banner text: Establishment Demagogue.

I stepped past the open door and walked inside toward a wooden island. There were stacks of folded T-shirts, screen-printed with obscure slogans that could have been puns. I heard a noise to my left and, turning, saw two men behind a register counter. One was Jose, who seemed curiously enfeebled now that he was wearing glasses. He was seated leaning back with a pen in his mouth and his hands behind his neck, and from where I stood, his eyes came just over the countertop. The other man, standing behind a monitor, wore a beard and a collared shirt. He looked to be in his thirties. The wall behind and above them was much like the one in the stairwell. I was almost lost again in the symbols and slogans when Jose spoke up and waved me closer.

"Harlan, I want you to meet Cody Wilson. We had him speak at the LL meeting."

"Mr. Wilson in the flesh. We meet at last."

He shook my hand over the counter.

"Welcome," he said with a warm smile and his arms out wide, "to the literal underground."

"A pleasure. Do you mind if I take a look around?"

"Please."

I browsed the rows of books, whose shelves were decorated above with masks, old propaganda, and pencil sketches of Ben Bernanke and Tim Geithner. I spotted titles like *The Creature from Jekyll Island*. *Anarchy, State, and Utopia*. In the back hung a poster with the black-and-white profile of Roddy Piper from the film *They Live*. Its caption: "Brave New Books. Out of Bubblegum since 2006." The store's logo was taken from the Great Seal of the United States—an all-seeing eye overturned.

The shelves to my left held Jim Marrs books and Alex Jones DVDs. I spoke to Harlan as I walked, asking him more about the shop.

"The real surge in popularity came with the Ron Paul moment in oh-eight."

I stepped into the meeting hall at the back and leaned forward a bit to see the stage and chairs.

"Is this part of that Libertarian Party office I saw across the hall?"

"No, man, that's our room for our meetings and speakers. They can use it, of course. We keep it pretty busy."

"I've lived here for over a year now and had no idea. Does Austin have any other radical bookstores?"

"Yeah, there were Marxist ones from the past that used to be more influential. But these days we're really it. And I'd say even from the beginning we've been a target."

I looked over to him. "And why do you say that?"

"Do you know about Brandon Darby?"

Jose smiled and looked at each of us in turn.

"What. What's the deal?" I asked, not quite sure if he was serious. If any of this was.

"Aw, man, it's a long story. This kid is supposed to be a radical leftist. He runs with the left anarchists for years around here. Fast-forward to the Republican National Convention in oh-eight; we find out he's an FBI informant. There's a great documentary on it. He got these two kids arrested on domestic terror charges for making Molotov cocktails."

Harlan had my attention.

"So, one of his old friends wants to testify against him in the trial for these kids, and his story is that Darby himself was always trying to blow things up or provoke violence in Austin. He says one time Darby tried to convince a group of kids out here to attack my bookstore!"

He was speaking with a laugh then.

"But why would anyone want to attack you guys?" I asked.

"Yeah, that's the question. And there's a couple ways you can look at it. One, these leftists just think we're part of the patriot movement, you know, or they just hate the individualist strain of libertarianism. Maybe the FBI just wants a convenient way to set it up. And knowing Darby was working for them all along, it's totally consistent with the Bureau's pattern of using their provocateurs to actually *do* their dirty work. And what are we doing here every day? Teaching people about sound money and trying to live without the State. Maybe to the FBI that's a real threat."

I stood wondering.

"I'm sure you see what I'm saying," Harlan said. "And another thing. This guy was supposed to be a leftist, and now he's Tea Party working with AFP?"

"And did you know we're a hate group?" Jose joined in.

"Ha! Is that right?" I looked to Harlan and then around me at the rows of books. "You're a hate group?"

"Yeah. Look it up. We've been on a Southern Poverty Law Center watch list for years now. Now tell me there's no mission creep over there."

Hm, I thought, it was true! This bookstore was a hotbed of hate. All this pulp for homegrown extremists. Men who liked to return to the words of Washington, Jefferson, or the other lunatics in the *Profiles of Perpetrators of Terror*. This place was surely a mecca for those lunatics who draped themselves in the flags of the violent ideology of self-reliance, and who sneered out privileged and insane slogans like "Individual Sovereignty" and "Consent of the Governed." Watchwords of slaver paranoiacs if there ever were.

Luckily Homeland Security's Dallas County Fusion Center was on the case.

I walked back to the counter, past the island of T-shirts, the booklets on fluoridated water, and the natural foods and soaps. On the shelf near the register sat a slight stack of dime cards. Each bore the figure of a grinning Death. His arms were wide and his speech captioned: I Support Everyone's Troops.

I didn't know it then, but I would share some of my happiest times in Austin at Brave New Books. I'd also develop real friendships with the people I'd meet there. I remember when we read the Dread Pirate Roberts interview there and celebrated. In 2012, if someone asked you, "But how do we know crypto and the Internet are winning?" you told them about the Silk Road and getting long in bitcoin.

"So, what's your next step?" Jose asked. "Will you keep going?"

"I'm meeting Mike Cargill in a couple of days."

―――――――

Mike was a club sponsor for the Longhorn Libertarians. He was a black, gay libertarian who ran the only gun store to make it into the Austin city limits after 1975. It's still not clear to me which of these is the more amazing feat. We had met the night of my speech while I was on my way to meet Mr. Liberty, and walked together from the campus Tower plaza, past the Littlefield Fountain, to stop outside a sorority house. He asked what motivated me while the nearby sorority security guard walked in and out of that giant house like a tired old wind-up toy.

I told Mike that I wasn't sure at the moment. At first it had started with a simple desire for political mischief.

We turned toward the guard.

"Do you think he even sees us, going on like that?" I asked.

It was a Saturday when I visited Mike's gun shop, Centex. Inviting me in, reaching for and holding up a handgun, he offered to show me anything from his inventory, but I declined as graciously as possible. I wasn't quite here for that. I was looking for a safe place to begin our work. After Mike stowed the weapon, we walked back to his office. Across the hall, a group of five or six was taking a concealed-carry class. When Mike got a call, I noticed he had two cell phones at his desk. He spoke on one, vexed about his own recently failed run for office. He checked texts on the other.

Mike soon invited in his number two, a young Asian man with an athletic build who held himself with stiff composure. Mike introduced us, explaining what I wanted to do, but the man had no words for me.

Without looking my way, he stood over the desk and typed at Mike's computer while we sat watching him. I sat perturbed on the couch as he walked out.

"Uh-oh, he doesn't like you," Mike said with great pleasure.

"I'll remind you both that I was invited here."

"Well, he's my partner. You two are going to need to get along if it's going to work here."

"Okay," I said, standing.

"Let me see that." I stretched over his desk, as Mike turned the monitor toward me to show the website.

"No, no, no, this is milling," I said. "This is CNC for rifle components. I'm working with a different technology and different concept. We're talking about a polymer pistol with an open-source license."

"Relax," Mike assured me, "I get it."

Still thinking about my unkind dismissal, I said, "Guy can't have a conversation? It's almost like he's a miserable prick."

"I'm on your side, man." Mike chuckled.

Looking up from both phones, his thumbs poised over each screen, he continued, "Now how big is one of these machines you want to use?"

I placed my hands against my head. "Yeah, I was looking at your side rooms, and . . . well, before that, let's talk about the legal situation. Could be a printed pistol is a National Firearms Act weapon. So, we'd need the tax stamp on top of your license."

Grinning fully, Mike pointed to a framed piece of paper lower on the wall. "So, if you'll let me talk . . . I'll show you I just got my SOT. That's it right there. Just put it behind glass."

He tapped the space on the wall just below where he'd hung it: Special Occupational Taxpayer. The special stamp the government issued if a licensed FFL had paid to manufacture, import, or transfer NFA weapons.

"How long did it take?"

"Maybe three weeks! Not bad at all. Though I hear applications pick up for ATF in the fall. So, we're ready to go, right?"

"Well, even then we're not home free." I sighed, and leaned back on the couch. "There's still the problem of the Undetectable Firearms Act."

"Never heard of it."

"It's a long story." I gave him the condensed version of what I'd picked up while researching the law. "So, back in the day, the *Washington Post* ran an article about the new Glocks and how Gaddafi was buying them up to get his spooks through US airport security. Plastic pistols. Handgun Control Inc. makes the Glock its first big issue. They lobby Congress to ban the Glock as a setup for wide-scale handgun bans."

"But Glocks aren't plastic," Mike said.

"Yeah, full of gunmetal, everyone involved knows it. But the NRA gives the issue up. The HCI bill doesn't affect industry or the public. Nobody makes a gun with less than seven ounces of steel, so why *not* ban guns with less than seven ounces of steel? Perfect compromise. NRA throws HCI a bone. Passes without incident."

My phone rang. "Is there a place I could take this? Maybe twenty minutes for an interview."

Mike showed me to a stock closet in the back.

When I returned, we walked under the awning to the next door over. The goods inside were laid out in open bins and under flat glass cases, like this was some kind of swap meet. Mike invited the older man in the store to come outside and meet with us. He was huge, tall, and red-faced, a good old boy in suspenders who nodded at me as I shook his massive hand.

"Well, what are you boys doing?" he asked roughly.

Mike pointed to me.

"This guy wants to get his FFL and deal with the ATF."

The old boy shook his head no. "Nobody wants to deal with the ATF."

I smiled expectantly.

"The F Troop. Never met one who wasn't here to make trouble."

Mike joined in. "They say the ATF is where to go when you can't get any other job in law enforcement."

The old boy stood looking off at the traffic. "Almost every guy with a weird look is them," he said, turning back to us. "Saying something stupid. They're here to trip you up. End your business. Put you in jail. But it's slower after that trouble at the border."

"That's not so bad, though, right?" I suggested. "Don't deal with the creeps and the spooks who walk in."

"But it's worse than that," said Mike. "The trouble is more subtle. Say you come into my shop to buy a handgun. Maybe you want two. If I sell you more than one in a five-day period, I'm compelled by law to fill out a form on you and send your info and the serials to the ATF and the county. You're on a list and they don't want me to tell you I just put you on it."

I listened to half a dozen more scenarios like this one. These businessmen were upset at being agents of the court. By being granted a license to sell firearms, they had to be part of an apparatus they wished to otherwise resist. Better that I not go their route, they counseled. I stood with them a while longer, speaking over the roar off Highway 290, but soon made for my car.

"I'll let you know if I think we can do it here, Mike. I really appreciate you inviting me out to see the place."

He smiled as I turned, and spoke to me.

"Hey, if your car doesn't start the first time, you run."

––––––––––

The week weighed on me. From my chair I watched the light leave my living room. Restless, I biked into the dark and toward the lights on Guadalupe. I hid out at a kebab place until they put on the president's victory speech, whereupon I set out to wander again, riding to a hamburger joint named Players on MLK. It looked beaten and old, and like I could trust the yellowed lights in the kitchen and the worn and oily order window. I began to calm.

After ordering, I walked to the soft drink fountain and was stunned by the light emanating from the largest flat-screen television I had ever seen. Before it was a squad of students in blue club shirts, transfixed at the sight of their victorious commander. They sat bunched together awkwardly at a pair of undersized tables, hands and bodies tremoring. Deflated, I took a seat in the back to watch the paradisiacs as I waited for my food. A grizzled old man and I shared a serious look, as if to affirm the poet. *Too many are born.* My jaw throbbed from the fillings I'd received earlier that afternoon.

When they called my order from the window, I found the tray slowly, and back at my table looked at the burger with increasing disinterest. A text from an old friend in Arkansas ribbed me for buying all those last-minute Romney contracts on Intrade. "Looks like the poor socialist beat the rich socialist!" I studied the all-too-many enjoying their victory in real time, cheering their fresh subjectification along with the human props on the screen. Far away, in some other city, the thin man at the rostrum said something pointless. Each round of the televised crowd's eruptions was the very jingle of the death horse.

After a few minutes more, I departed my medicated company. I found my bike in the blessed dark and managed to get halfway up Guadalupe before my legs quit. I walked the bike slowly then, listening to my ragged breath coming over the sounds of the quieting street. I was overtaken by the slow and isolate cars, and into the air a drunken undergrad threw a broken cheer.

PART V

Danger

I found it hard to even hate-tweet about the election. Foregone conclusions have a way of working on you like that. Along with that sense of resignation, I had DD and my classes at the law school to contend with. The semester was winding up, and though I hadn't spent much time focusing on my assigned reading, final exams were nearing, and following them, the winter break.

Maybe once exams were out of the way I'd figure out how to actually make a gun out of plastic.

Through Mike Cargill I'd been given a few leads about shops with the equipment and expertise necessary to get me further in gun printing. It also helped that they were, if not completely sympathetic to or supportive of DD, intrigued enough by the proposition to speak with me. But first I thought I'd go meet with the machinist Daniel Fisher again. Something told me I should take him up on his invitation to head out his way.

That Friday I drove west for Fredericksburg. I moved beyond

the ringed highways and amid the white slices in the limestone hillsides to where the country lay spilt like ransacked sepulchers. Those crumbled hills took me further out, past the empty crossroads at Johnson City and past the owners of horses, fields, and traditions. Seventy miles as the drone flies. I turned at a lonely stagecoach stop and broke the dust down an old road named Alamo. Navigating the cracking turns, I passed stands of blighted oak, stricken black and white like ashy newspaper in the evening glare.

Past rows of barbed wire, faded cactus, and shattered boulders I scraped over the drive to Daniel's house. It stood modest and simple, with green wooden eaves and a front doorway open to a metal screen. At a remove and up a slight incline was a garage with a corrugated roof. I stepped out of my car to the rising cricket song and stood in the long-cast shadows from the tree line before walking toward the house.

"Guess you found your way all right," came a voice from behind the shadow of the doorway.

I squinted as I approached. Daniel spoke as the screen yawned wide with a springy creak.

"Hey, buddy."

At the door he shook my hand, a strong handshake that let me feel I could trust him. He inclined his head to indicate that I should step in. His home seemed like one large room bisected by a couch. The front walls were lined with a stereo, a computer desk, and stacks of DVDs. In the back was a kitchenette and a bar with access to a sliding glass door through which I could see a concrete pad and out again to the hills and horizon. He let me tour the space alone as he gathered up a box beneath a table near his bar. He must have had time to slip into his bedroom as well, because when I turned, he also carried two rifles by their slings.

Still holding the clattering box of tools and components, he asked me to sit with him. I watched him sift through the box and spread out the day's paper and some magazines. He laid a rifle across the tabletop near a wooden fruit bowl. The other rifle he stripped and, after popping some metal pins, pulled free its black lower receiver to clink down at our hands. As he worked, the wrinkles on his forehead and above and around his eyes faded, as if his mind didn't need to regulate what his hands were doing.

I saw in the box an EOTech sight, a bolt group, and some type of ruggedized barrel sheath. He had collapsible stocks and grips in desert khaki. As I watched, I listened to the wind moving through the trees outside.

At last he held up the stripped receiver.

"So, this is machined aluminum. You can see in places it's pretty thin."

I turned the cold black piece over in my hands. The magazine well showed the stamp of a spider. Its finish was slightly rough and grainy, and it faintly sang as I ran the calloused edge of my finger against it. There were three colored stampings around the selector switch.

"Safe, semi, auto? Is this an automatic?"

"Ha! Well, no. They just ship them like that. I guess you could say it's an option, though."

He reached beside his chair and from the box brought up another receiver.

"Personally"—he paused to let that word sink in and to add

emphasis to what followed—"I'd most like to see how close you can get to something like this."

The receiver he now held was dark gray, and I imagined it giving slightly to my touch.

Daniel assumed the tone of a teacher. "Now, this is a commercial polymer lower. Glass-reinforced nylon."

Our conversation began to wander as we waited for his brother to arrive. He mentioned a 5k run near Kerrville where you could carry your gun and asked if he might have a printed lower for it.

"Don't want to be carrying too much weight if I'm running."

"Makes sense to me." For his bulk I hadn't taken him for a runner.

We heard his brother's car clatter and pop down the driveway then and walked out to meet him. His was an old BMW like my own. He gave a quick wave as he got out.

Followed now by twin sable kittens, the three of us walked to Daniel's garage.

"Cody, this is Eric."

"It's nice to meet you, Eric. You do design?"

Eric nearly squeezed one eye shut and then rubbed his chin before responding. "Well, basically. I work at a kind of security company. I have to get around pretty good in SolidWorks."

"Right now they're working on a biometric scanner," Daniel added.

"Oh," I said. "Is that kind of stuff for a government contract?"

Eric seemed embarrassed.

Noticing the barbed wire his brother was stringing up around the subject, Daniel stepped in. "Hey, and his boss is a pretty funny guy. Remind me to tell you about him."

Daniel sent the garage door clambering up, and we stepped inside. The rear was filled with metal shelves, each stacked with surplus ammunition cans that read .30mm in yellow letters.

Daniel sat in a rolling office chair beside a bulky laser etcher that looked like the front of an old car. Beside the laser etcher was an aged washing machine covered in oilcloth and gun barrels. I picked up a plastic bucket of threaded barrel adapters, and Daniel pointed at them.

"Right now I finish those at the shop. The boss doesn't mind."

I leaned against the washing machine and watched him and Eric.

"Get this," Daniel said, nodding toward the etcher. "It still runs on Windows three-point-one. But I was thinking when you bring up a piece, we could try etching on it."

"Sure, that would be cool." It was a fun thought, joining old and new technologies that way.

Eric walked around and behind me, picking up a compact AR rifle from a shelf.

"Is what he's got there a short-barreled rifle?" I asked Daniel.

"Well, that's a good question. The barrel is fourteen inches, but I've built this one as a pistol."

"You can make an AR pistol?"

Daniel and Eric smiled.

After a few more minutes of the brothers' show-and-tell, it was time for me to take the lead. They knew what I'd proposed to do in general, but I wanted to be clear about my needs. Before we could make the leap to producing a complete weapon, I thought it best to start producing a few receivers. We could print that part because I'd seen it done, and we'd perhaps begin to learn how to bring ourselves the rest of the way.

"Say I want to bring this lower I make out here for you to finish, Daniel, and for you to help with revisions, Eric. Can you give me a parts kit?"

I was looking down at a new Troy magazine in my hands, charmed by its fish-scale pattern.

"Also, soon I need a place to film shooting it. The BBC and CNN keep asking if they can come down and film something one day. If we can get a workflow, can they come film here? Clear off the pad, we shoot out back?"

Without looking at one another, they nodded.

Later, we stood around a raised Porsche in some uncertain stage of restoration. Still talking, we soon walked outside to watch the failing day.

———

Under the streetlights back on Seventh, I texted Jackson and Brent: "Let's do it."

Jackson had cleaned up Michael Guslick's CAD blueprint for printing the AR receiver. With Daniel and Eric on board to assist with testing and modifying the files after production, I was ready to begin.

After hurtling down a dark and empty Highway 1, I met Jackson at the shop. When I arrived, my headlights passed over him stepping out backward from his Jeep. We walked blindly to the ailing old desktop beside the printer. The screen flittered as it came to life, and I stared. A progress bar jumped up on the monitor, and a light from the print head split the darkness. Jackson too was lost in watching it.

"The same heads HP uses for their inkjets," he said, pointing. "I mean, it's the same stuff."

"Which is more dangerous?" I asked. "The printer or the weapon?"

I drove home in the early morning, the whine of the Objet cutting through all my thoughts.

When I returned to his shop after daylight, Jackson was at his desk.

"Hey, I even cleaned it for you."

He had left it alone on a folding table, against which it glowed a spectral, sickening green. I'd brought a gun case, the first hard-shell case I could find on a closet shelf at McBride's, and stood at the table cutting out a foam footprint for the piece with my pocket knife. Jackson and Brent walked in as I was at work, taking turns praising the thing. When I got it out to my car, the light over the dashboard multiplied its eerie effect. I drove to Fredericksburg cast in a new pallor.

It was late when I made it to Daniel's house, which was filled with guests. When I got there, the interior light came through the screen door, making a welcoming path. I stepped quickly over the gravel, which jumped and shivered as I approached the door-step. Daniel introduced me to his wife, Heather, once I was in-side and seated among them. She was gentle and lovely, with long black hair, and she frequently stepped back around the bar to check on the food she had prepared for everyone. I met a young man in glasses next, who looked about my age, named Tyler. He told me he'd left UBS in New York for a trade and an honest living. Daniel had asked him to come work with him at the machine shop, and though he knew nothing at first, he was now every bit a machinist. He wasn't in the business of making gun parts on the side like Daniel was, but they shot and hunted together all the time. Not having brought food for the get-together, I popped open the hard case and left it there on the bar like a puckish gift.

"Ha-ha! No way! You cut the foam just for the receiver?" Daniel asked.

Tyler took it in his hands. "This is tight. It's got a fleshy feel."

Daniel held it next. I admitted I was too nervous to touch it much yet.

"I keep thinking it will be like wax or crayon," I said. "Don't want to grasp it too tight."

"I can't get over the detail. Look at that," Daniel held it back out to Tyler, pointing to the piece's rear. "I figured we might have to finish it with some hand tools, but the threading in the buffer ring is just fine."

He looked down and reached for another receiver, motioning to me.

"This is that nylon lower I showed you the other day. Now compare the buffer towers."

We set them beside each other and I took a few pictures with my phone. I was still in awe of what I'd brought.

"You can see the clear differences in thickness and give here," Daniel said, pushing at the printed buffer ring.

Tyler's girlfriend arrived later on in the night, and with her Canon she took pictures of us all. At one point Tyler called her "love" and I felt a real pang of envy. The man must have really been proud of the life he'd made here. She passed the camera around and we all took turns playing with it.

"I like this one," I said, showing a moment she had caught of us all. "Please send this to me tomorrow."

My favorite conversation piece at this little party was the mammoth antitank rifle beside the couch. A Finnish Lahti with a top-mounted magazine as big as a gas can. The whole thing sat on skis. Daniel broke out a slender-bodied AR-57 upper receiver for our build out.

"I saw Guslick used a twenty-two conversion kit," he said. "We'll use this."

He next held a handful of blue-tipped rifle cartridges. "I think going with the five-point-seven is definitely riskier than testing with the twenty-two, but you're getting closer to a true rifle test this way. What we'll shoot will look like a rifle."

After we did a dry run building out the gun, using other spare parts that Daniel had on hand, the result was surprising. The whole assembly looked unusual and discolored, but the heavy, polished upper was seated just fine on the lower. The upper's particular ejection port meant we'd need to use a magazine with a nylon sock riveted around its walls for catching the spent casings that would leave the gun. While still feeling a little unconvinced by it all, I had to admit that what we'd built was quite handsome.

We finished the night telling stories about feral hog hunting.

"Oh, yeah, they've totally taken over. They'll tear up fields. Kill dogs. We'll go out hunting them with night vision."

"What, like on ATVs?" I asked.

"No, that will scare them away. You go on foot. We'll get five or six a night. But yeah, you don't want one to get you."

"It's surprising how quickly a thousand years of domestication can vanish," I said.

And the room agreed.

Then I remembered reading about stray dogs on the Moscow city subways. In a city with an estimated thirty-five thousand dogs wandering the streets and left to their own devices trying to survive, the smartest of them had learned to navigate the complex transit lines, getting off and on at select points with the same regularity and intent as human commuters.

"Explain that to me," I said. "Man disappears on the pig and it becomes wild. He disappears on the dog, and it takes the subway."

In the morning I felt the chill rising from the floor. I climbed up onto my elbows from a quilted pallet, looking to the screened doorway, but my eyes couldn't open in the morning light. I tottered to the bathroom and then at the kitchen table sat in silence while I waited for Daniel to wake. When he was around, I stepped outside with the lower in hand. As he ran back and forth outside to his Geo, dropping gun parts under the back hatch, I stood just behind his garage, watching the weeds panic and the sotol sway all the way out to the tumbled uplands.

We rumbled down a back road near an old homestead. It bore its German name on a wooden signpost, and I asked Daniel about it.

"Used to be you couldn't get by in the town just using English. The people spoke Texas German, but in the last generation or so it's disappeared."

I was quiet for a while then. I thought of what it must have required to have made the passes this far west in the nineteenth century.

After we drove by a rusty shooting gallery swallowed in dark overgrowth, I spoke again.

"So, what's wrong with the trees?"

Daniel glanced to his left, toward the dozens of them that stood sagging like pillars of ash. "That's oak wilt." After a few seconds he spoke again. "Even beneath the healthy trees you'll find the rot out here."

I returned to my previous thoughts and then almost fell asleep. The sun was out over the rocky pastures of the Texas Hill Country.

We arrived at the machine shop where Daniel worked, and I was surprised to find it an inconspicuous metal shell. I don't know what I had expected. Inside were rows of CNC machines and an ancient lathe. The place smelled of oil. I followed Daniel as he found the appropriately sized tap wrench at his workbench. He switched on a lamp, and then using a type of hand tool that had existed for at least a century, he carefully turned the device to cut the internal threads needed to affix the handle to the back of the green lower.

I was delighted at the simplicity of the performance. "Let me see that again," I said.

In the back of Daniel's Geo we had stowed two rifles in halves beside their stocks. I sat with them as we traveled back out of town, and my head bobbed as I was again tempted to sleep. We headed to a ranch on Old No. 9, south of the ancient trace that ran to Grapetown.

Our host's name was Davies, Daniel told me. "And this guy has been reading everything about you."

We got out behind his place and made small talk, clapping together the rifles and loading them into the back of an ATV.

At midmorning, we all rode into the hardscrabble together. I rocked along holding the makeshift weapon, past the desert cypress and creosote. Toward a white and flattened eminence, we went on like mechanized Janissaries, the first slaves of a new and terrible kingdom. Before long we stopped and stood in the wind, and Davies directed us toward a group of rusted plates at a berm, there bent and welded into a mutant figure. A shape like the Old Ones might have left on a rock wall for a coming race to scrutinize.

The pale sand ran with the gusts as we loaded the uneasy green piece. I turned windward to hand Daniel my phone and saw the sun like a cold burst in the faultless sky. I walked as he began recording, and brought the rifle to my cheek. It felt top-heavy, and as I looked down the sights to the target, the air ran stinging over my ear.

The rifle spat. At my shoulder it pumped and flexed like a thing alive. I took it down in my arms between the rushes of wind and inspected the piece's back, inviting Daniel to step to my side. We pored over the ring of material wrapping the rifle's buffer tube, where Guslick's printed lower had broken. I looked up at the rusty analogue ahead, feeling troubled, then glanced back to Daniel, pointing to the buffer tower as I offered it up to him.

"You can empty it when I start recording."

I held out my phone in the windy blast.

He fired five times. When the rifle clicked, a misfire, he brought it down from his shoulder and the green thing belched its innards, buffer and spring and bolt, all at once to the dust.

We threw the stock and pieces back into a bin in the bed of the ATV and had no appetite to shoot the other rifle.

Davies kept his hands in his pockets. "Well?"

"I'm not sure," I said, unthinking and a little anxious.

On the drive back to Austin, I called Sean Kubin to report on our mixed results.

"Do you put the video up?" he asked.

I repeated the response I'd given to Davies. But by then I didn't mean it. Sean and I both knew I'd post the video. I was satisfied with the work. The lower receiver had held up for a few test shots. It wasn't perfect, but it had, however briefly, worked.

Regardless, it was time to restore a little illusion to the world.

The posted video was like the terrible coincidence of the idea and the real. We didn't have to wait long for a response.

The bloggers, anxious midwives of the spectacle, were sure to carry the story, but it was like they wanted it over as soon as possible. To quickly pronounce the event's lack of worth and resupply some meaning, they opted for humor, denial, and criticism.

"The Wiki Weapon Is a Six Shooter," one headline went.

Sure it's a gun, but it's a "crappy gun," Rachel Maddow of MSNBC eventually offered.

I wasn't upset. If you'd asked me what was happening, I'd

have told you it was black magic. We were watching the chattering classes deal with the terror of an idea realized. What could they do but be mystified? This was the agony of the concept. I began wearing my sunglasses at night.

Days later, Guslick himself sent me an article from *Roll Call* magazine, a press organ for the House of Representatives. The chairman of the Democratic Congressional Campaign Committee (DCCC), a representative from New York, had discovered that the Undetectable Firearms Act was expiring at the end of 2013. He put the legislation back into play shortly after we posted the video of the working receiver. He ran an admirable presser inside an airport screening area, where, gripping the podium beside the Long Island police chief, he said it was time to renew the "Wiki Weapon ban." I was charmed.

Discover him now, the career politician, in his ideal *mise en scène*. Standing before the security cordons and the imaging machines, he is a divine ward. Agonarch—judge and censor—imbued with the power to renew and remodel. He has no quarrel with the Order of Things, just the desire to make adjustments here and there. His pact with the Creator, you see, is to preserve the world as it was originally planned. To use his superintendence to make that design more intelligible.

He must separate what is from what can never be.

But the money quote was in his press release:

> Law enforcement should have the power to stop the proliferation of guns with a simple Google search.

And I had hoped we might be able to run out the clock on them.

Cory Doctorow, the Canadian-British sci-fi author, journalist, and blogger, issued a response to this move. His species of response was, like those of the bloggers with a similar digital rights position, certainly sound enough: the politicians couldn't really get their hands on 3D printers. It was right to assure people. But I thought the straight, pragmatic response missed the philosophical beauty of the scenario. Laws like the Undetectable Firearms Act and the proposed anti–printed gun bills to come were announced more as theater than anything else.

I hoped we could just laugh off government responses like these. What were the odds they would even yield policy at this point? I tried not to think of it again.

After the presentation I gave to the UT libertarians, I had befriended the photographer from the school paper. I asked her over one early December night to have a quick photo session with the broken rifle. She photographed it in the breezy dark outside my doorway. The timed flashes struck the upper receiver's rail, which on her camera's display seemed to come out like the teeth of a sinister saw. A young reporter I had kept up with by phone said he thought a picture he'd seen of the unassembled lower looked skeletal, and something about that stuck with me. I brought the green and broken rifle to a *Wired* photo shoot downtown the next week and saw the mongrel thing suspended on wires. An absolute object. Superconductor of unmeaning. The room was quiet, haunted even. An assistant tasked to mind me found her voice caught when attempting a question.

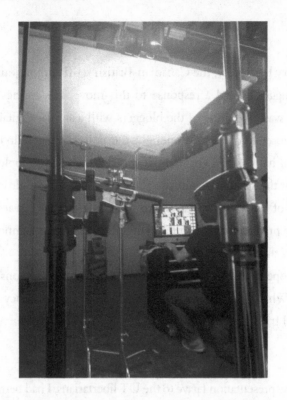

I was so impressed by this that afterward I asked a local proto-typing firm to produce two more lowers for me, and to do them in white.

That week I noticed the death threats had stopped.

The Perry-Castañeda Library on the UT campus appears to have broken from the earth around it like one of those outrageous concrete monuments on the Alexanderplatz. To its fourth floor I hauled the books on metalized plastics that I had taken from the chemistry library. The smack of my backpack echoed around the musty stairwell. I cut across the stacks and settled into a row of wooden carrel desks along a back wall and, after a five-minute negotiation with my laptop, was settled. I hurried back and forth through paper notes, the textbooks, and a list of articles from academic databases. The news in 3D-printable materials that month was a composite developed by researchers at an English university. They had produced a conductive material for printing made from a carbon black filler.

Carbon black. A petrochemical product from crude oil and coal tar, ethylene residue, and vegetable oil. Readily available and inexpensive, it was blended with a printable, thermoplastic matrix from cheap modeling plastic and the result christened *carbomorph*. The researchers had printed simple circuits and thermogauges into common objects. They asked you to imagine a coffee mug that displayed its contents' temperature. I'd ask you to imagine a trigger mechanism. From the name to its method of inexpensive production, I was enthralled.

In this new material I saw another confirmation. Its advent was like the signature of some elemental arcanum, complicit with forces not at all interested in human affairs. *Carbomorph*. Born from incomplete reactions and destructive distillation. From tar and pitch and heavy oils, the black ichor that pulsed thermonous through the arteries of the very earth.

"The world is filling up with detonators," Ben once told me, speaking of the devices used to trigger explosives. They proliferated on their own mysterious course, flowering like lily of the valley.

He seemed to have already understood this revelation entirely.

Ben was sometimes bored, given his rampant zeal and intellect, with Wiki Weapon. But I wasn't so tired of it now. Witnessing how all of this had begun to evolve, how the receiver had taken on its own afterlife in images, was fascinating. I was being surprised every day. But being restless, Ben had for a month now hounded me with other ideas.

One of these ideas was for a handheld urea convertor. Piss into it over a few weeks and have your own little stock of potassium nitrate. At this point everything we were about seemed to circle back to this inexorable theme. One that couldn't be allowed to shine through, I reckoned, but was still there should you look: the world was irreducibly weaponized. And down to our basic organism, so too were we.

We even pissed explosive.

I wandered through a scientific database on my laptop. The universities understood this unfortunate idea as well, I thought. Despite the odes to humanity, they treated all this impounded knowledge, these digital articles behind layers of gateways and passwords, like so many canisters of fulminate. They outsourced their work product to publishers who licensed it back to them. Worldwide, they paid curators to hold their stockpiles fast within proportionately weaponized architectures.

And why?

The university student need only look out the window. Find the parapets and turrets. The stone chapels and baileys of the old fortified towns. Someone told me there were fourteen libraries here at UT. Fourteen little castles. In times of rebellion, an insurrectionist raids the public armory. Shouldn't the good rebel find these academic repos valuable? Couldn't Occupy have started here? The locked caches of all this schoolman's work were calling. The tiled roofs and cornice details of these tuition mills seemed to cry out for the siege.

Aaron Swartz must have understood the problem in these terms. Maybe only a one-man siege was required. He had the right idea, regardless. Do you recall the video of him in the Massachusetts Institute of Technology server room? He didn't wear a balaclava to hide his identity. Just a pea coat. Does he feel like he's being reckless? In the video he still has a bicycle helmet buckled to his backpack. He leans out of the frame, picking up all the data he's just boosted from the university network, perhaps mere hours from releasing into the public domain the aggregate knowledge of centuries.

He moves almost unhurriedly, like he thought they'd let him take it. Like all that talk in the seminar room about the commons was for real. Maybe he thought they'd forgive one of their own. Because hey, sometimes history needs a little help.

It was a university discourse that had also ultimately diverted the anger, so sweet and decorous, of our friends the Occupying. In trying to triangulate against Wall Street, they had, at their peril, invited in the professoriat and the graduate horde. If there were leaders with articulable grievances, they took a back seat to the primetime poeing and to the mouthers of total-state, humanist garbage.

Maybe next time, we raid the industrial base's research universities. And maybe next time, we consider with suspicion those universities as neutral social institutions. Even now they prepare new fleets of psychonauts, ready for that final frontier of civil rights action. To defend the cold monster, to report on their fathers, and to weekly deliver unto us the lexicons of political equality.

My cell phone's vibrations knocked me out of contemplation.

"When can I see you again?" Ann texted.

We had fought the week before. I studied the phone for a bit and laid it down on the old desktop. I looked around and started to pick up the books.

———

That night she wore fur boots for me. I met Ann near campus and drove her out to the Salt Lick at Driftwood for dinner. Her coat was thin and she held herself close to me as we waited outside to be seated. I remember her dark cheeks and close smile. She was researching a trading algorithm for her PhD and was sad that by the year's end she would return to Thailand. Without using the words, she asked only that I keep her laughing.

And so we laughed. At the barbecue, and at how she hadn't known she was ten years my senior. At high-frequency trading firms that had never had a bad day. And we laughed at America.

What a splendid circus. An idea of a nation preserved in the light of its financial and political models. A system of silent majorities, economic patriots, and plunge protection teams. Four years after global financial collapse, we were each of us condemned to an endless Recovery Summer—its permanent open-market operations, Fibonacci fades, and momentum ignitions. It was a time when everyone was long, no one was left to buy, and there was nowhere left for us and the markets to go . . . but up.

I lifted my cup to Ann and her project. Surely we had finally reached that final plateau of prosperity: a reality perfectly reconciled with its concept. *Go and tell the bath-salted things of the night they've good reason for cheer. There's another rally in stawks.*

I told her I had once seen the Commodity Futures Trading Commission (CFTC) chief Bart Chilton in the security line at

Clinton National Airport. You'd have known his hair anywhere. We approached from opposite directions, staggered just enough away from each other in the miserable human switchback. I leaned in when we was beside me.

"Bart Chilton? CFTC?"

He started but looked nonetheless pleased.

"Hi there."

"You don't know me, but it's a pleasure. My name is Cody Wilson. I'm in bitcoin."

"Oh?"

He moved his neck back a bit, his face more expressive than I had expected.

"And how's that going for you?"

"I have to admit it's going pretty good."

He looked over his shoulder and back to me as we shuffled around a belted stanchion, and then spoke:

"For now."

After dinner I watched her pick a bottle of wine from the restaurant shop, feeling lucky we could spend our own stolen season together.

Avoiding even the thought of school, I sought ferment more and more. I spent hours staying up into the night. I found a *Torrent-Freak* story about a patent firm securing the rights to a phone-home software for 3D printers. Remote denial for printing the politically incorrect shape. I wanted time for long musical audits to find that perfect ostinato, the right prelude or string sequence to intimate the antihuman and irrevocable movement of my organization. I bought a Virtual Private Network with bitcoin and set up extra communications with Tormail. And if you'd told me both services would soon vanish at the hands of statesmen, I'd have jeered.

Like the oldest mass-market subversives and blasphemers, I searched for my own printer's mark. When it seemed that the world was asleep, I let myself enjoy a sense of possibility and truly felt like I had absolutely nothing to lose. In the daytime I drove around town to haggle with prototype shops and pick up the next revision of the blueprints for the lower emailed straight from Daniel's brother Eric. Overtaken again by night, and in moments of near delirium, I thought I could just glimpse something else and still without a name. Something other. On the weekends I headed west to break the new pieces, a lonely but joyful outrider.

I suppose even then I still believed in a negative liberty. A "freedom" that, if anything, meant the absence of external coercion. I entertained myself with a chapter by Leoni referencing the bishop of Winchester, and found comfort in a book by DeLeon on the American's indigenous, spiritual anarchism: Once an English governor had come to the Pennsylvania Colony to find his meetinghouse empty and in advancing disrepair. It's reported another rode horseback through the street and asked two colonists, traveling from the other direction, to yield the road for him as he passed. They told him to screw off and yield himself. What, did he think being governor made him better than them?

I was still committed to "rights talk" when in early December 2012 I gave an interview to a reporter for *Popular Science* magazine. I thought it was likely he wanted only the tech aspects, but that wasn't where we went on the call. Near the waxy agave plant at the street corner outside my apartment, I walked in circles, on the phone. The afternoon light did nothing against the lingering cold, and from behind my glasses I found the dog sun between the power lines overhead. To promote the project I struggled to make the best use of the American idiom.

"What does it mean to be serious about civil rights?" I offered to the reporter at the other end of the line.

"Yeah. Yeah."

"This is part of why Sandy Levinson called the Second Amendment embarrassing. There was once this—admittedly it's paradoxical—this republican faith in the body politic. Liberals become conservatives when they talk about the Second Amendment. There's none of this prudentialist talk about social cost when you mention amendments four, five, six."

I was holding out my fingers in the middle of the road.

The best I could say then was that America was a failed but worthwhile experiment. A miracle from the finest moment of liberal thought. Proof that foolish political experiments, be they compound republics or plastic guns, still had their fruits in the animating contest of liberty. I wanted to think of the American as a good-natured conspirator against power. Or at least indifferent to the powerful, more often than not happy to frustrate those globalist pigs who might wheedle him out of his freedom. Americans were a people who, even if they didn't have the words or the politics, had known their republic as a positive anarchy. A freedom as Pierre-Joseph Proudhon described in his *Solution of the Social Problem*:

> Neither liberty subjected to order, as in the constitutional monarchy, nor liberty imprisoned in order. It is liberty delivered from all its shackles: superstition, prejudice, sophistry,

stock-jobbing, authority. It is reciprocal liberty, and not the
liberty which restricts; liberty, not the daughter of order, but
the mother of order.

But then even kings were republicans. And I had long sensed
the boredom of paradise.

_____

On a brick plaza under the giant raised highway on Research, a tat-
tered shepherd watches his carts by night. Ann and I drive beneath
this titanic ossature, replaying my new favorite interview. The
headlights and neon rake over my windshield. Our shadows cycle
forward and the spoiling colonnade is ablur as NPR's Bob Garfield
asks me about bitcoin money laundry over the cab speakers.

"That sounds like terrorism!" he mews with cultivated alarm.

Ann and I laugh maniacally.

"Ah! Jesus Christ," he had muttered between takes in the studio, his quiet curses sailing sweetly into my headset at KUT. "I'm
pretty sure you'd be better off in a cell."

I had looked up from the table to exchange a nasty grin with
my glassed-in producer, who shook in gleeful silence.

I take a call as I watch the bleached backbone overhead, the
flung ruin of some leviathan, rush into the darkness obliterate.

Ann looks curious. "What is it?"

"It was *Wired*."

At twenty-four I would be named one of the most dangerous
men in the world.

PART VI

Jarhead Angel

On December 14, 2012, I followed the sidewalk up the hillside and made the steps to the white forecourt and the covered stone walkway flanking the law school's rear entrance. I had stood atop it one afternoon the year before to watch the clouds of smoke cross the street and take the swale below. We began looking at the sighing live oak differently that month. The once-green dressings between the chopped stone houses, the boughs which before had leaned so romantically across our quiet lanes, now betrayed in their dry whisperings something fatal. I remember the fires and that fall, and looking back at the Spanish entrances above the walk to see—perhaps for the first time—this place and the claustral order it sheltered for what they were.

Ready to take my Corporations final, I crab-walked between the higher rows in the lecture hall, a thin plastic binder tucked under my left arm. The student proctor wrote the time on the whiteboard and in the next minute her partner began passing out paper exams. I had just seated my backpack when my phone lit with a text from Andy Greenberg at *Forbes*:

> So will this affect DD's plans?
>
> I don't know what you mean.
>
> Newtown, CT.

I looked up and across the rows around me. The room passed into stillness as each student settled with their instruction packet.

Andy's question could mean only one thing, but I'd deal with it on the other side. I stashed my phone away for the next five hours.

———

As I left the exam room, I read the texts amid the crush of students, who, likewise released, darted and spun in complex turns toward the concourse and the bathrooms. Under the covered walk and through the atrium, I flipped through my Google news alerts. I jogged for the steps at the corner of the outside courtyard and took the granite stairway beneath the giant, sprawled oak. Two of my classmates had caught up from behind and asked me how I did.

"Well, I passed, anyway. Hey, you guys didn't hear about a shooting up in the Northeast, did you?"

They hadn't. Well, not the best question for polite company anyway.

The sky was mottled and a slightly sapping breeze stirred. A man with a printer in Liberty Hill had offered to meet me today. I headed home to gather my things but upon arriving was surprised by two figures standing outside my door with lights and camera gear. I swerved into my parking spot and cut the engine as its creaking blast bounced off the apartment's stone walls.

"Wow, sorry, guys. I guess I forgot you were supposed to be here. Were you waiting long?"

I had my key in the door. The photographer helped his assistant hitch up a longer bag and then he looked back to me.

"Nah, just twenty minutes or so."

I let them in behind me to set up their lights and I headed up the carpeted stairs. I threw down my bag at the corner of the bed and stepped into the bathroom, where I caught a look at the purple rings beneath my eyes. I stepped in toward the mirror and blinked a few times, my right hand at my cheek. When I paced back downstairs, I was in the tightening grip of some new unease. Maybe it was just hunger.

The older man said they were doing work for the AP. He asked me to sit where I might normally, and I moved a stool out to be seated at my kitchen bar. His assistant opened the blinds behind us to let the light from the overcast sky flood the austere little room. They took a few stills and I moved my elbows back to the counter's edge. The assistant soon had the smaller camera panning four of the lowers we'd made. Black, blue, and clear. And a green receiver, glued together at the rear. I turned the black one over in my hands for them. It too was split at the back and the buffer ring was in a few chips I had left near the other pieces. On its test day, the rifle had slid off the back of Daniel's car. We never even shot it.

They went on filming as I slowly replaced one receiver and took another from the countertop. This one was likewise broken. I wouldn't be able to shoot anymore until after exams, and I'd returned the upper receiver and most of my working rifle pieces to Daniel. The green receiver was slightly yellowed now from weeks of exposure to the light. It was smudged and abraded near the face of the grip mount. Its cleanest spaces were where the blotches of epoxy sealed over the tears in the buffer ring. It seemed covered in a thin layer of grime. I tilted the screen of my old ThinkPad to help the older photographer match the frame rates, and began to manipulate some part files in virtual space in one of the old file viewers I found. At last I told them I had to leave, and they began to pack.

"Seems you could have printed anything," one of them ventured. "So, why guns?"

In another ten minutes I had left my building without apologies. I had one more task to complete before I could really consider everything that had transpired that day.

When I rolled into Liberty Hill, the clouds overhead sailed low and fast. I parked in a lot beside a taqueria to call Ben, listening to the thunder gusts between the flat tones of the ringback in my ear.

"Hey. So, what have you heard about all this?"

I wandered from my car to a concrete parking block, kicking a jutting piece of rebar as Ben answered, and looked up to watch the trembling grass in the open field behind the lone building. The sky was slate and the air was thick with the smell of the dust before rain.

"I heard it was a Sig a lot at first. They keep talking about a Bushmaster AR now, but that might have been left in the trunk," Ben said.

"It was an AR. There's an energy to this one. Has to be."

"I noticed this feeling as well. From what I've seen on Twitter, the usual suspects are outright excited."

"Let me know what you can find out. I'm about to go see a guy who's got an industrial printer."

The clouds ran in darkening streaks behind my glasses. "You know," I said, "we may have less time at all this than we thought."

I drove into town then, past a pair of shopping centers and a signboard with a ragdoll pistolera. A Girl's Guns, it read. The strip was dotted with gas stations and supply shops. I turned right after a railroad crossing and took a narrow road to Brian Bauman's house. Parked beside a line of mailboxes, I waited for him to text me the code to the community gate, which read Mustang Mesa.

The wind rushed through the tall grass.

When I found his place, the garage door was open. He greeted me outside and invited me in through a laundry room. His children were eating quietly at the kitchen bar in the half-light while his wife apologized for the mess. We walked into his room and sat at the desk before the computer, where he had pulled up a video of Alex Jones:

> Throughout history, every authoritarian system has sought to disarm its serfs. And the same is happening in the United States. In every case, governments have used school shootings to—

"I was just telling my guy," I said, as Brian stopped the video, "we have less time than we think to get this done."

Brian told me he watched RT's *Keiser Report* and listened to 90.1 FM. He talked about sound money, and I asked if he had heard of bitcoin. Preliminary shared bona fides established, we turned to business.

"Well, I have a background in the industry and I've been following you guys for a while. Pretty much from the beginning. I saw you print the AR lower. It was an Objet you used, right?"

"Yeah, a Connex series. ABS-like was the material."

He leaned back a bit, puzzled. "Do you mean PolyJet?"

"Ah, yeah, PolyJet. But I wanted the closest thing I could get to ABS."

"It looked like Objet stuff. I had seen what you were up to for a while. I reached out once I saw your video with that green receiver."

"Hey, it was all I had access to then, man."

"Well, yeah, I saw that and I thought, Well, if they're just doing Objet, I could help them do better than that. The best materials for functional applications are thermoplastics. I think SLS would be the best for this application—"

"You don't mean metal powder?"

I had cut him off and watched his expression cloud over for a moment.

"Not exactly, but I don't have SLS technology anyway. I saw you had your FDM printer confiscated, so you know what that is. But what I do have is an SLA machine. Have you heard of that?"

I shook my head no. Brian looked pleased at that.

"Traditional stereolithography cures using a solid-state laser. It's at a wavelength to cure both epoxies and acrylates. I use an epoxy-acrylate hybrid with impact modifiers so you get the kind of toughness and resistance you might expect from a usable part.

And we can approximate the tensile strength of thermoplastics like ABS."

"I mean, great," I said. "Right now, I just wanted to get as close to ABS as possible. I figure that's the target."

"What do you mean?"

"Well, this whole project doesn't just have technical goals. It's even more constrained by a political goal. So, we want to see if we can print the gun, yes, but can we do it in the materials and with the technology most widely available? What most people will have access to—that's ABS."

Brian launched into some explanation of the pros and cons of ABS, referencing a materials sheet I hadn't yet seen.

I remembered in that moment the day I had biked to the College of Engineering. The pitch of the street coming off Guadalupe is aggressive. I locked the bike to a signpost and, once through the basement entrance, wrested some papers from my backpack as I searched in vain for an elevator. A student at a corner chair inside just shook his head no. I punched a door's metal bar and took six flights of stairs.

Sweat-through and pale, I rambled down a pair of halls and entered the departmental office, finally speaking with a pleading look to the chair's secretary.

"I'm looking for Dr. Seepersed, but I can't find her."

I entered the professor's office winded but blusterous. On a metal filing cabinet in the corner, I spotted a grainy geodesic ball, like the remains of some ancient brainless halfling, neither plant nor animal. For our entire conversation the professor maintained a look of fear and sympathy and suspicion all at once. Was this a stickup?

"Have you even used an extrusion printer before?" she finally asked. "I would think ABS wouldn't be able to stand the pressures involved in an application like that. You're talking about an explosion."

The good professor handed me a red, printed T joint and suggested I read an article on layer adhesion. And with that I was dismissed.

———

Brian Bauman stared at me, his expression shifting into modes I couldn't place; the hardened flint of his downturned mouth was jagged.

I waited. "Please, continue," I said.

"Well, I wanted to reach out and help you get closer to your goal."

He brought me back through to his garage. We parted the vinyl flaps hung over the corner doorway and reached the printer's preserve. It seemed as large as a carnival dunking booth. Like a two-toned kiosk, with little red piping that reminded me of nothing but the old Nintendo Entertainment System. A status screen was mounted on an aluminum arm beside the machine, and a rack with a little keyboard hung below that.

Brian stood with his hands on his hips.

"In a day or so I should bring that computer from my room out here to manage the builds. But I can show you a bit more of what I'm working with."

He keyed a few commands and I heard the low whine of invisible motors.

"Okay, now look in the build envelope."

As the build tray within the printer rose, odd forms atop it pierced the surface of a milky bath that filled the space. The fluid drained off the forms gently, and I stood struck in that peculiar moment, the one after things are produced and before they have a name.

I took a second to speak. "We're going to keep building receivers, but what do you think about trying rifle magazines as well? And how do you feel about TV cameras?"

He laughed. "I guess I'm not against them."

I believe we were friends from then on.

––––––––––

Sandy Hook had the chatterati apoplectic. The blogs had passed judgment. Like it had been that summer, it was time again to end the Second Amendment.

> All of it for the sake of an obsolete and currently stupid inclusion in the Constitution of a "right to bear arms"—a right that no longer makes any sense except to people who make money selling guns.

> We outlaw the sale of many poisons because they can be used to easily kill people, but the most insidious killing devices of all, guns and bullets, are available everywhere because in the 18th century there were backwoods people killing animals for food.

> Fuck you, NRA. You guys are fucking murderers.

> Today, we don't need prayers. We don't need thoughts. We need action. We need to politicize this, and we need to politicize this now. Fuck everyone who isn't ready to talk about gun control.

I read the *Washington Post* editorial board's "Time to Talk about Gun Control" unable to contain my disgust.

Salon had a school shooting liveblog.

> Today I logged onto Armslist.com, a kind of eBay for guns, for the first time. It didn't ask for my name but it did require me to confirm that I wouldn't hold it liable for anything I do with its products. The first page I saw displayed a .223 caliber Bushmaster rifle, similar to the one reportedly used in today's shooting.

Okay, so they wanted a fight.

———

I would go back to testing new receivers in Fredericksburg that weekend. Each was costing about three hundred dollars to produce now. Between trips to the ATM to pay everyone, I stopped by J&B early Saturday morning to ask the guys to look for any kind of AR magazine files online that we could turn into prints. No need to reinvent the wheel.

After an hour on my way west, a state trooper pulled me over. I sat silent as he looked through my passenger window and at the seat full of envelopes, hard-shell cases, and plastic rifle receivers.

"Where you headed?"

"I've got a meeting at KNS Precision at two."

"And what do they do?"

They were a machine shop, I told him. And I had an appointment that I didn't care to miss. I wouldn't be on my way without a ticket.

Parking out back at KNS, a shop tucked well away down a

country road, I walked around the tall grass and into the air conditioning. Their modest shelves were half-empty.

"You guys have any AR lower parts kits left?" I asked a clerk.

They had two. The man behind the counter pointed them out to me. As I checked out with him, I saw the manager in the back at his computer.

"Hey, have you guys heard of the 3D printed gun stuff?"

The manager looked at me only briefly.

"What's that?" asked the man at the counter, handing me my bag and receipt.

"Well," I said, leaning back into the door now, "just google it sometime."

The newest printed pieces tested much as before, working without incident until a failure near round one hundred. Once again, I took the long drive home, which was now feeling longer. From out of the blue I took a phone call from a former Magpul Industries employee. A major player in the industry. The guy offered to make DD a magazine. He asked only what I thought it was worth for him to do so.

"It guess it's worth . . . three hundred to me?"

"All right, we've got a deal."

The billowing clouds to the south were aligned like a team of beasts, hitched in order to ride the hills.

———

Five days after the massacre at Sandy Hook, I sat at the Kerby Lane Café on Guadalupe with a team of Germans. The place was bright and enamel white. We were five. The camera crewmen were all playing with their mugs and unsure of what to say. They gaped at me as I took my own drink, amazed the gun printer could sip coffee without bursting into flame. The crew had been at Red Rock or Gruene the day before to solicit some old guy to say, "From my cold dead hands." Christian, the youngest man at the table, had made the introduction on behalf of ZDF television.

I remembered one of the last things he had said to me on the phone. "And because we are publicly funded, you can be sure we are not biased."

I watched the screen above the lunch counter to our left. CNN's Don Lemon was live at some corner stop not far from the scene of the murders, a miserable hysteric. It was too loud in the diner to make out what he said, but you know pleading when you see it. I made a note to hunt for the audio when I got back from the trip ahead.

When we were ready, we all drove out to pick up a lower from Brian at Mustang Mesa. He and I had a pretty smooth workflow by then. He printed a lower or two the night before with one of his other builds. In the mornings he'd remove the rest of the pieces but keep the gun parts on the platform and lower them back beneath the gooey bed of resin. When the cameras showed up, we'd do a little interview, film the machine, and finally lift the pieces out slow, letting them ooze and shine like Terminators in miniature. It was a choreographed fever dream.

After cleaning up today's lower and thanking Brian, I led our German friends on the long drive west to the airport at Fredericksburg. We met Daniel and waited at the Hangar Hotel, watching the empty fairgrounds from the parking lot there. Leaning against the hood of my car, I enjoyed the stillness, the plain enormity of my surroundings. The crew walked out to a tower and watched the single props come in. Daniel and I caught up. As the sun came lower, Tyler arrived.

"All right, there won't be too much more sun and these guys have to get on a plane back home in a few hours. Daniel or Tyler, any restrictions these guys should know about?"

Daniel addressed them. "Film anything you like. I just ask that you don't film his folks' gate when we get to the property," he said, pointing to Tyler.

"Is that all right?" I added.

"Of course."

"Yes, understood."

We caravanned out to Tyler's place near Kerrville, a ranch hidden in the cleft of the surrounding ridges and freestone. Soon it was dry going, and the weeds and thistles brushed against the panels of my car's undercarriage. Placed between us, the Germans drove slowly, as if unsure of their wayfellows and reluctant to see what might come raking over each new bend. We drove down through an iron gate and settled in a hollow.

From my trunk we pulled two plastic trays of receivers, stocks, and springs. The Germans, still in their SUV, had backed up and turned. Daniel scoffed.

"The one thing, the one thing they couldn't do was record the gate. Look at 'em."

They filmed us with an almost lusty curiosity. And we regaled them as we installed our parts kits and buffer springs.

"I saw they're selling Pmags for a hundred dollars now," said Daniel, as we built our rifles together.

"My buddy at a regional distributor said they sold all their magazines in a day. One day."

"And why do you think this is?" asked the director, to no one in particular.

"It's panic buying," I said. "We know the laws are coming."

An hour or more of shooting had finally broken the receivers. As before, they all cleaved in two through their rear takedown pins. I was displeased, considering all the time and money these shows required, but the Germans liked it well enough. Daniel and Tyler showed the crew their other black rifles and offered to let them fire some rounds.

"Would you shoot?" Daniel asked.

The crew looked among themselves, at first furtively and then with a fixation that seemed to help them form a silent pact. Since no one was looking, yes, they would briefly shed their German-ness and have a round with the forbidden. Their barrels flashed in the afternoon light. We gave them our ear protection and watched their delight with each report. Even the director, after popping off a few, turned his head over his shoulder and gave us a smile.

During the first weeks of that semester break, every weekend I drove out to Fredericksburg, each time with as many receivers of as many designs as I could afford to print. Among the batch that next Saturday was a clear receiver done in PolyJet. Daniel put in the parts kit and held it out to Tyler to watch the hammer move over the pins inside. Onto the piece he clapped an upper I hadn't yet seen.

"I wanted to try something different today," Daniel said to me. "I think you'll like it."

He showed me the rifle cartridge. "This is 300 Blackout. I had to mess with the gas a bit. This round is subsonic, and I've got the upper silenced."

"You want to watch this," Tyler offered.

Daniel pulled the trigger in rapid fire. Over the slight breeze I heard the quick clicks from the rifle and, in a brief moment, the quiet thumps across the hollow at the berm. I looked back to Tyler, feeling my brow rising.

I ate with Daniel and Eric on the old main street in Fredericksburg. Eric had been to a wedding the weekend before.

"The guy I'm with starts talking about Defense Distributed.

He says, 'I even heard they're testing out near Kerrville.' And I was like, 'Yeah, that was me!' The look on his face!"

I showed them then a YouTube video of Rachel Maddow:

> People have started to make lower receivers for AK-47–style weapons at home. Using a file that you can download on the Internet. You can actually download it—right here I have one on my computer which makes me wonder about the next time I have one of those things where NBC comes and checks my computer.

We could have kissed her.

Halfway back from Fredericksburg, and coming down from the hills, I got an email from Michael Guslick: "Well they finally did it." Thingiverse.com, Makerbot's public repository for sharing and exchanging printable design files, had taken down Guslick's lower receiver file and was removing still more—silencers, grips, and stocks. They were rooting out the gun files.

I pulled up next to the pump at a Shell station to call my contacts at *Wired* and *Forbes*. Until that moment, I just thought we'd upload our work, when it was ready, to Thingiverse too.

"I thought maybe one day we'd have had a whole portfolio there, you know?"

"What will you do now?" Andy asked.

"I'm going to call Haroon, I guess," I said, referring to our web guy. "Guslick offered to send his files over and recommended a few others do the same. I think we'll just make our own site for the banned content. A place to put it all back up for now. The island of misfit objects or something. We need to send a message that the Internet routes around censorship."

By then you could say Makerbot was the flagship Maker company. And by now I had made up my mind about their "movement." At first it seemed like maybe we, the DD crew and the Makers, were fellow travelers, mining a similar vein of the bedrock of the American spirit of self-reliance and independence. But all their talk . . .

This carnival barking about the "Next PC Revolution," "The Third Industrial Revolution." These startup ringleaders, bloggers, and "early adopters" were together a union of peddlers of middle-class ideology. *What would you build? Can you imagine the future? Don't feel lost, just look at the graph.* You are here. Breathe in. Now.

"Feel for yourself that sense of achievement and exhilaration when you see before you the finished object of your own labor, and how that object has in turn made you more than you otherwise had been."

But nobody here truly meant to give you a revolution. "Making" was just another way of selling you your own socialization. Yes, the props were period and we had kept the whole discourse of traditional production, but this was parody to better hide the mechanism.

We were "making together," and "making for good" according to a ritual under the signs of labor. And now I knew this was all apolitical on purpose. The only goal was that you become normalized. The Makers had on their hands a Last Man's revolution whose effeminate mascots could lead only state-sanctioned pep rallies for feel-good disruption.

The old factory was still there, just elevated to the image of society itself. You could buy Production's acrylic coffins, but in these new machines was the germ of the old productivism. Dead labor, that vampire, would still glamour the living.

As December ended, I packed up for Arkansas. Near the I-35 on-ramp and a public storage building, a billboard overhead read Don't Mess with Texas. And it simply frustrated me. Words like those could embolden or underline the distance that separates us. They could be a motto for a homeland, or a threat to make against the common enemy. But in this country, even in Texas, they could only play as raw, administrative injunction: *Pick up your trash. Good subjects don't interfere with the State's preserves.*

Somewhere on I-30, outside Dallas, I stopped at a hotel. Shoeless, I walked the dark and frigid parking lot to the clammy tile lobby, where sweat pooled in the corners of the inner set of glass doors. While I waited at the reception desk, I noted the black plastic vesicles, like polished spiders' eyes, dropping from the ceiling.

My room smelled sour. I turned the dial for the fan on the AC unit and sat for a bit at the edge of the bed, not moving. Listening to the night outside, I didn't feel like sleeping. Past the thin, drab curtains, I heard the passing wail of engines, all joined in harmony like a ghastly choir of the apostate.

I pulled out my phone and saw I had overlooked an email from Ben. Below his signature he attached a comic strip with six blocks. An angry young boy in a T-shirt and black hair hurls a shout. His brows are dark and furrowed securely in a righteous anger he knows is justified by the moment. He cries: "How many children have to die before you support gun control?!"

In the next block bursts a sparkling radiance from heaven. The boy shows his surprise and apprehension. He shrugs a little under the light, and in the next panel a helmeted angel in camouflage face paint begins a winged descent. The angel is wide-eyed, wearing a toothy grin. He carries a miniature harp and a paper card. The boy's expression freezes. The wide-eyed angel then smiles with a ferocious blankness and, fluttering just over the boy, leans in with both hands to offer the card. The boy squints uncertainly but accepts it all the same. He watches the jarhead angel rise back to heaven before finally glancing down to the card that reads ALL OF THEM.

Walter Benjamin once wrote about an angel of History who floats above a scene of devastation with outspread wings and staring eyes. Where we perceive an ordered chain of events, he sees a single catastrophe ceaselessly piling wreckage upon wreckage. The angel would like to stay, awaken the dead, and make whole what has been smashed. But a storm is blowing from Paradise, and its fierce winds catch in his wings with such violence that the angel can no longer close them. The angel's face is turned toward the past. The storm irresistibly propels him into the future to which his back is turned, while the pile of debris before him grows skyward.

Benjamin said this storm is what society called progress. Bound together by the concept, we had romanticized the slaughter bench of history. I doubted then if any idea still united the world, but in the West surely the "program" was a candidate.

I saw in Ben's jarhead angel the angel of Evil. Where we see the avoidable, the intelligible and preventable, when we cry out for another system and rational program to end our misfortune, the rays of catastrophe send the angel to us. And he's an American angel, true to our oldest tradition of direct revelation. Only ask, and he comes with pitiless enthusiasm to provide your answer.

The spasmodic eruption of violence is preferable to the price of total pre-vention.

That night, in a fetid off-ramp hotel room, I figured we are, each with all our "only ways" and "at all costs," the boy who won't accept his consignment to the unreasonable, unalterable eruption of disaster. We would rather not understand that when the rationalization of violence does indeed come, it will be on the wings of a total liquidation. So sayeth the jarhead angel. If the Old World had perished by the idea of progress, so would the New by the program.

I tried to call Ben but got nothing. He often ran off to the Ozarks for weeks on end. When I woke the next morning, I dropped my bags into my trunk and made the drive through Titus County and to New Boston. In Arkansas the golden feather grass, rusted-out billboards, and the geese at the retention ponds were welcome sights. North of Little Rock the power lines shone like spider's silk in the declining sun. I made my way beyond Pleasant Plains and to my grandmother's house.

Late at night on Christmas Eve, Ben texted back a photo. He was dressed in a ski mask and fatigues, kneeling under a softly lit Christmas tree. Who took the photo I could not guess. But craning his neck to peek beneath the brilliant, plastic whorls, the merry guerrilla had discovered an old Krinkov. He popped his gloved thumb in delight.

PART VII

John

The day after Christmas, Senator Dianne Feinstein released a bill summary with a reserved gusto, a quiet solemnity that she hoped spelled finality. It was good that we were dropping the bromides and the double-talk. In ninety-four, when the Assault Weapons Ban, a part of the larger Violent Crime and Law Enforcement Act of 1994, was passed, a prohibitionist with rolled eyes could still be heard to say, "No one is talking about taking away your guns."

Now we had a simple three-page list of what had to go.

Just before New Year's 2013 I flew back to Austin for the day for an interview with the ATF, who recently seemed inclined to give me a manufacturing license. I had to have a business address, of course. But luckily J&B was renting me a cramped corner of the shop for about a grand a month. I arrived at our offices a couple of hours before the ATF agents would be there to inspect.

"AKs, thumbhole stocks, everything. This time they're going

for a one-feature test instead of two or three. Does your rifle have a threaded barrel? Assault weapon. Banned."

Brent and Jackson listened as they carried the extra desk into the back office. They cleaned out the front office so that more than one person could sit down, and so the ATF might believe that a person could work here. A brown Labrador ran panting through the office doors and back and forth between us.

"I appreciate you letting me stay another month in the place."

"As long as you need to get the license, man. Can you hand me that?"

I handed Jackson a stack of papers from the chair beside the desk.

"Hey, this is it," I told them, still working to get some enthusiasm. "It's just like ninety-four, only this time the AR is the country's favorite rifle."

My insurgent excitement couldn't find an audience, and I declined to follow the two to the garage door, which they lifted high to let in the brightness and crisp, cold air. I stood before the desk where I had first met the boys and took in the newly bare walls and the filthy, naked floor.

"All right, boss. Best of luck." Jackson slapped my arm and walked with the dog to his Jeep. He swung himself up to the cab and Brent entered from the other side. As they pulled out, Brent waved good-bye.

In the next hour, two large men in collared shirts and name tags approached me outside the J&B shop. My eyes followed the bound folios they carried.

"I'm Agent Turner, this is Agent Murphy."

I shook the hands of the men from ATF, making sure to keep eye contact with each man in turn.

"Won't you come in?" I asked, surprised by how pinched my voice sounded.

"Today we'll just inspect the shop and go over your checklist. Nothing too bad," Turner said smiling, and then eyed his partner, who seemed to sigh as he began opening one of the folios.

And so began the longest formal interview of my life. A stack of papers. Phone numbers. Attestations. Where and how to post the Youth Firearms Safety Act. And then a dreadful panic: from out of nowhere the terrible challenge of fighting the need to sleep.

"As for your business area, Mr. Wilson," Turner continued. "Okay, it needs to be secured against all other points of access and have an alarm. Okay, do you have an alarm?"

The three of us rose and toured the back of the shop.

"You'll need decent safes," Turner said, searching with his eyes and talking slowly, like he was making a calculation or was a realtor assessing curb appeal and livability. He looked dubious about what he was appraising.

"When we come back here, don't let us see the guns in the same room as the business, do you know what I'm getting at?"

I tried to make the mental note, but my brain had gone beyond numb. When they at last walked back out of the shop, I had lost the spring in my legs.

Unsteadily I escorted them to their car.

Turner spoke as the other agent buckled up in the passenger's seat.

"All right, look for your FFL in a few weeks, I'd say."

At least I thought that's what he said.

———

A few days after my interview with ATF, I stood at a will-call desk, having a difficult time turning the onion leaf pages of a product catalogue. I felt the man opposite me look me over with impatience. It was one hell of a catalogue.

"All right, I'll take this one, then."

I left the Grainger supply store with a pair of calipers. I took Highway 1 south and watched the moving train beside me in the stormlight.

At home I slapped some printer paper on my coffee table and set it under the thirty-round Pmag I'd used for testing most of the rifles we'd built. From a quick trace I began accurately dimensioning the magazine's every feature. The work took me all through the night. Brian had set me on this task. Once I had the dimensions done for him, we could send them to an industrial designer he worked with in Louisiana. He'd then work them up into a CAD model and we could start printing AR rifle magazines.

Faced with the obvious prospect of new federal gun laws, we could worry about patent infringement another day. Besides, Magpul, the maker of the Pmag, was having its own problems out in Colorado with the lifestyle socialists in the state legislature. What would set DD's development pace now was the progress on Senator Feinstein's proposed bill, S. 150, the Assault Weapons Ban of 2013 (AWB 2013), which, if passed, would soon put rifles like the AR, not to mention its magazines, out of reach.

I could never figure Feinstein. The force of her famous distemper for the popular ownership of arms seemed matched only by her muscular defense of our warfare-surveillance state. She, and a few others like Representatives Michael Castle, R-DE, Alcee Hastings, D-FL, and Mark Kirk, R-IL, had introduced bills to reauthorize the expired 1994 ban as far back as 2003. While they were at it, Senator Frank Lautenberg and Representative Carolyn McCarthy, East Coast liberals both, worked on similar legislation, which would never get out of committee.

Still, there was something about Feinstein's particular doggedness that made me curious. She kept a much harder position than even Nancy Pelosi's at the time.

> "There has to be a national conversation," said Ms. Pelosi, who was active in the House in 1994 when Congress passed an assault-weapons ban that has since expired. "The safety of our country cannot go as slow as the slowest ship in the House of Representatives or even the United States Senate. If we come out of the Newtown experience and all we do is talk about it and not have a result," she added, "that would be a dereliction of duty on the part of us in public office. We must find a place where we can come to agreement on this."[2]

But maybe Pelosi had gotten to the heart of the matter. If a binary existed in the gun debate, it existed only to illuminate the

---

[2] http://www.nytimes.com/2013/01/09/us/politics/after-newtown-congress-must-act-pelosi-says.html?_r=0.

correct way to salvage a political principle. Both sides believed that political power resided with those who controlled the use of force. Libertarians were suspicious about the growth of that power, while liberals seemed convinced it was dying and needed life support. But neither side believed that power was never real in the first place.

———

Rain would fall that whole week. I had stayed in touch with the staff at *Vice* magazine since the Stratasys printer was taken and told a young producer named Erin that the first week in January would be a good one to come by. In another week or two I'd be off to Europe to raise money with Amir Taaki.

Erin and her team got to my apartment early, and I took them right upstairs.

"What's with that?"

The younger of the two cameramen pointed behind my computer's monitor to a paper I'd framed like an achievement. The top read, "Social Security, what's in it for you."

"Why did you frame it?"

"I like to look at it, wanted to preserve it. One day I'll give it to one of those old country nostalgia restaurants in the Neo-Confederacy where the people can gawk at it while they eat."

I showed them my own black rifle, Individual Mandate, an AKM from Izhevsk, imported and remanufactured by a firm out in Las Vegas. And how they were drawn! And yet how they shrank away! The younger cameraman crab-walked around it in a semicircle, as if the gunmetal vibrated to the specific frequency of his spine. He held his camera out between him and the rifle as a buffer, as if he were on some deep-water expedition. Was he filming it or shielding himself? Here was the fulfillment of all that internalization of expectation. The sites of social enclosure worked! Perhaps he'd been too long in school.

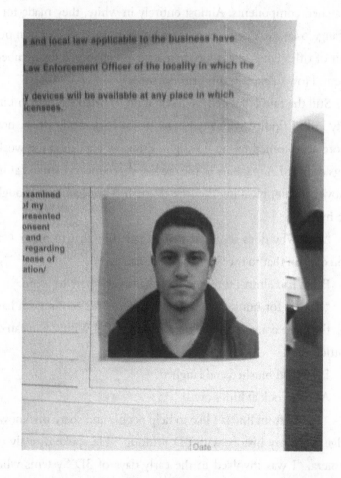

Downstairs I opened an old Soviet spam can of 5.45 ammunition and saw beside it an old note I'd written while on the phone with Ben that read "Factory Discipline." Erin caught me considering it again for a moment. I wondered what it meant to her. As her crew went on filming, I kept trying to sneak my Zero Hedge coffee mug into the shot.

Next we moved to my bar, which was by now a graveyard for broken receivers, aborted magazines, springs, and their mismatched components. Almost entirely in white, they made for a strange ossuary. The team asked a lot then: for a description of a pair of rifles lying splayed in their stages of shattered dismemberment. How to explain this brittle armory?

Still the rain fell when we made it up to Brian's garage in Liberty Hill. I fiddled with my phone in the back while Brian, now more accustomed to the limelight, dutifully explained the workings of his SLA machine to the crew and producer. I smiled at his showmanship, recalling the first journalists we had ever brought up here.

"And why does someone need a rifle like that to hunt? Can you explain that to me?" one of them had asked.

Brian had almost thrown up his hands at where to begin.

"It's not for hunting!" I had cried then. "We're not even having the same conversation. This is a battle rifle! With it you can do battle!"

Brian had blushed and laughed.

Ah, but look at him now.

"The bottom line is I like to help people and share my knowledge from my history with 3D printing." He spoke directly off camera. "I was involved in the early days of 3D Systems when Carl Deckard would roll into the lab in his powder-filled chair playing the harmonica when I was working the third shift and going to college."

He stood surer in the key light.

"I've seen an evolution of the technology that I fell in love with, and I'm seeing all these new faces. This is a good thing. Even though this idea is not really new, you can see innovation is never stagnant."

We sat together at his workbench while they filmed the laser in the SLA machine.

Erin continued to talk him up.

"You're seeing this moment because of the expiration of old patents. 3D Systems had been the first to market with the invention of stereolithography, or literally 3D printing. Like the abuse of laser patents in the early days, 3D practiced the 'art' of submarining patents by extending their claims back to the original patent priority date."

She was nodding.

"When you have new technology, it's easy to say, 'We really meant to say W,' based on a previous claim description 'XYZ.' Because not many people were experts in the field, it was easy to continue research and literally extend the patent life. But luckily this practice was outlawed in the mid-nineties. And now most of the old SLA and SLS patents can finally expire."

Erin was taking notes.

"SLA and SLS?" she asked.

"Stereolithography and selective laser sintering. Two of the basic forms of rapid protyping. Remember, 3D printing has been around for a long time to produce prototypes—nonfunctional solid parts. Now we're in the era of making functional objects. So, those old patents have been around for nearly thirty years. They had a nice little monopoly there for a while. As for fused deposition modeling, what you see with Stratasys, RepRap, and Maker-bot didn't follow this practice and became available even sooner."

As the *Vice* crew were packing their gear in the garage to go, Brian shook his head, held in some kind of reverie. He spoke softly and without looking at me, like he was finally seeing something he thought he never would.

"We all talked about printed weapons back then, you know. Working on this stuff. We all talked about desktop printers for the masses." He smiled brightly.

At nightfall, I took the camera crew to J&B to watch the Objet begin its first printing of magazines. While they set up their gear, Jackson and Brent picked my brain.

"Hey, were you ever contacted by a guy named Travis?"

"Oh, wait . . . you know that guy! This is a guy whose first email is to tell me my fifteen minutes were up and it was time to stop messing around and turn what we're doing into meaningful change. A Super PAC."

"Yeah. We went to school with him." Jackson said. "It came out the other day that we were working with you and he was like, 'I'm going to do it, I'm going to talk to him.' We were like, ehhh."

Jackson summed it up neatly, "Yeah, we hate that guy."

After some handheld shots of the Objet's piercing blue light and its movements to lay down the early, filmy footprint of the coming receivers, the *Vice* crew sat me in front of an old muscle car amid the open shop.

"Tell us what you were saying earlier about history and synthesis," Erin started.

I looked at her nose ring and black hose. The two cameras set up to her right. She asked me to speak Evil.

The world is choking on its realized dreams, I told her. Total fulfillment, perpetual growth, the satisfaction of every desire. The end of History. Globalism's positive destination turned into a murderous finality. In *this* world, then, the only remaining wells of power are in incompleteness. Reversion. Disunion.

No world can ever be truly realized. No system can ever reach its total perfection. No political philosophy can stamp out difference and violence and becoming. It will all fall back in on itself.

"Show them that," I said. "Use their signs and words and their technology and show them. Challenge them to stop it. Invite them to use all that might and, if you're lucky, watch it all begin to suicide."

I couldn't stop myself now. I was playing the only cards I had left.

"These planners think they can take us back to the gun bans of 1994, and everything can be perfect forever."

At the next line I saw them all look at each other with wider eyes. Erin would turn her head around to the crew.

"All I'm saying is no, you can't. Now there's the Internet."

I returned the following night to J&B to pry off the first magazines. Jackson directed me without looking up from his work.

"Yo, they're still on the plate. Didn't finish cleaning them yet. You're welcome to."

"Yeah, what do I do?" I said, now in the room behind him.

"Take them to the back and into the cleaning box. The pressure washer."

After I placed the parts in from the side of the plastic box, I stuck my arms through the two glove ports and had my nose against its plastic screen. I stepped on a small pedal underneath the stand upon which the box rested, which drove a spray through a jet nozzle resting just under the murky rinse still contained in its tank. I worked at the pieces with the sprayer, watching the support material slough off like broken skin. The sludge collected in the rinse like a bizarre, silicate afterbirth. I could hear Jackson ask about me from the shop floor, and I walked out to him. He was resting on his back under an old BMW.

"So, I'm going to have to get rid of the place soon, man. I'll be moving out of here in another month or so. Don't know where you want to go, but you'll need to go there."

"No kidding."

In the other room we heard a splattering. The seal in the bottom of the washer had broken. Jackson kept on just as casually, pointing from under the car.

"Hey, there's the mop."

The spring semester had begun, and again our grades were late. Back on campus I learned I'd managed only a B in my Second Amendment class. The universe was probably trying to tell me something; regardless, I showed up for the first day of the next round of classes to be a good sport. My three o'clock three days a week would be Professional Responsibility. Before our first lecture, I tore the shrink-wrap off the casebook and read the assignment in the law school basement near the mail room.

Ah, a new edition.

It read like doxology. I remember being stunned a man could

write the concepts in that book and support himself through an entire career.

When the class started, the professor asked a simple question: What is a professional?

"Someone who has a fiduciary duty to the public," a lickboot delivered from the back.

Regardless of the projected haughtiness of the student body, there was still a deep-set desire to toil here, I figured. We all had it. An enthusiasm for indebtedness and new servitudes. Worse, we enjoyed the ethical ideology of our masters.

Eight years through with loan forgiveness. Only two left? Oh, thank you.

While I attended law school I said we were the acne on the ass of Capital, ready to take the bit for the joys of officeholding. I sat that psychological siege another forty-five minutes, yellowing in the light.

"So, you're coming to class again?" a friend asked when we were out.

I left the building with him and a guy named Mike. We shared commercial outlines.

"You seemed bothered in there," Mike said.

I scratched the back of my neck and started in. "Friedman said something a lot like . . . you should be able to pick up a lawyer at the mall."

We walked further and parted alongside Dean Keeton, where a wild vagrant now bounded ahead of us. He ran directly into a parking meter and spun 180 degrees, muttering that it hadn't hurt. That was the last class I attended.

One night I went to a Valero gas station on Guadalupe to get an Icee. As the machine finished filling my cup, its spray terminating in a colorful little stalactite, I just caught my reflection in the station's window. The attendant across the floor said something my way:

"Yo, are you talking to yourself?"

I stopped for a moment.

"I guess it's just that kind of day," I offered.

In the parking lot I turned up my stereo to play "Blade Runner Blues." Haroon called about setting up our new gun file sharing website. I stood under the blue-green fluorescent lights outside my car, trying to catch any glimpse of the Austin State Hospital through the trees.

"Why don't we do a sign-up process?" I said out the side of my mouth. "Work their desire like they work ours. The first question before they can get approval for access is Are you a *freeman* or a *statesman*? Freeman and they're in, and statesman just starts them down a dozen-step process."

We laughed and I squinted at the cars from behind my sunglasses.

"Yeah, how long have you been employed?" I jabbed my finger into the dark and toward the oncoming headlights. "Now provide your financials and references."

That week we finished the website and named it *DEFCAD*, a mocking challenge to the idea of a securitized world of *any* defense condition. We had a two-track sign-up like I had wanted, and we found people emailing fits:

I selected statesman. When can I get approved???

The next night I went to the Spider House café in Austin, where the Christmas tree lights and the lawn ornaments announced the seventh circle of hipster Hell. I was there to meet an engineer named John, who had volunteered to meet after I put out the word for more help on Twitter. The last time I had hazarded this yard sale for the damned was with Chris Guevara, a friend from law school, who had asked me here in August to discuss the legal implications of Wiki Weapon.

That night Chris and I had discussed *Bernstein*, software as speech, and guns as software. If I publicly shared a CAD file for a gun on the Internet, if I purposely developed the file to be put into the public domain, was that not protected speech? Was software about guns the same thing as a gun under export law? What if guns were becoming speech? We wanted to nail our theses to the door of the law review. I figured the thoughts were a fine continuance of the trouble UT had already made for Second Amendment jurisprudence. A valentine for the school's esteemed professor Sandy Levinson, or just deserts for Lucas Powe's teaching right out of *Democracy and Distrust*.

At the Spider House I soon found John, a tall man in glasses with sandy blond hair, sitting alone at an isolated table toward the front of the house. In the red neon glow I could see he wore a light windbreaker and a Veggie Heaven T-shirt. His only other provisions for the freezing night air were shorts and sandals. As if the red glow off the Spider House was warmth enough. He told me he'd biked here.

We shook hands and I sat across from him in the cold seat of a metal chair.

"Well, I mean, tell me about yourself," I began.

"I just got back from New Zealand. It took me a while to find your email address. After Sandy Hook, I wanted to contribute to this conversation. I remember the original video you had about printing the gun. I just kept googling things like 'homemade gun,' and found you." I watched as John's legs bounced, whether it was out of nervous anxiety or to prevent the onset of hypothermia I couldn't be sure. "I watched your videos and found your Twitter. You said you were looking for help doing ballistics measurements. I work at a respected engineering firm in town and thought I should offer my assistance."

I didn't remember tweeting anything like that.

"First things first, I'll say I really don't care if you're a fed or not." I was smiling. At least as I recall. "Hey, as long as you do good work."

He laughed politely. But his eyes were still moving about me.

I asked about him and his life for a little while and then he got us back on track.

"Well, what was it you needed measured?"

I laughed. "We don't need it measured yet, because it breaks every time we shoot it!"

John looked put off. At least he'd registered some emotion. I relaxed a bit.

"About me, then." I paused while the waitress took the empty glasses from our table.

"Standard stuff. I think the US has become a state more absolute than any of the old monarchies of Europe. I'm disgusted by these massive House and Senate bills, where these psychopaths just wholesale transfer power over to the administrative state.

"With DD, yeah, I'll admit we don't know what we're doing. Sure, it would be great to measure some stuff on the receivers, but so far I can't even get them to stop breaking. If the goal has been a plastic pistol, my only intuition is that we create this illusion of progress while we figure out how the hell to do it. At least I know this much is working. Each of these pieces we're making, they're like talismans. More powerful props by which we operate in the media. If every week the printed AR shoots twenty more rounds, it drives this terrible, impossible narrative against the state-sanctioned 'progress' of technology."

John was really listening now. Lots to remember for his report.

"You've seen this guy in DC trying to ban homemades, right? We can handle that for the moment, but this project needs to be going somewhere."

"You want to make a printed handgun," John interjected.

"I want the *whole* gun, though. At first I thought we'd do it like WikiLeaks. Leak the gun. But now, with all these new bills and this progressive triumphalism, why not a freedom flight? Like the old FP-45 Liberator. A guy named Michael Dean brought it up in the first interview I ever did. There's one sitting in a museum out in Montana."

John was quiet for a bit. He still seemed upset I wasn't really ready for his help.

"Well, you want to shoot a machine gun?" he asked.

I was smiling wide and pulling at my jacket. "Sure. Hey, come to the parking lot and let me show you these magazines I just printed."

I took him around the corner and up a slight hill to my trunk and popped it to show the cardboard box inside. As I lifted the pieces to us, they lightly fogged up under our breath. They were backlit by the intense lights of a Chevron station across from us at an intersection.

"Cool, man," John said, all unease gone. "Let's go shooting."

We agreed to meet on the weekend.

On a Thursday, walking through a parking lot looking for Chinese food at a strip mall on North Lamar, I got a call from a man named Fountain at the *New York Times*.

"Well, I understand you were trying to make a handgun. I was wondering if you knew anyone else doing this kind of work or had any updates since the last stories I've seen."

"I do. But I tell you, I think we're about to do a new thing that's pretty interesting."

"And what is that?"

I was mean-mugging in the glass of a closed-up shop.

"Well, are you familiar with rifle magazines?"

A moment's hesitation.

"New York liberals like to call them clips," I added, then continued without waiting for him to respond. "I'll back this up. The talk on the Hill is about, at the very least, reinstating or making permanent an assault-weapons ban like the one in the nineteen-nineties. A feature of these bans and the debate around them always has to do with detachable magazines and their ammunition capacities. I assume you've heard this term *high capacity*."

"Okay, sure."

"Well, what can I say? You could see this one from miles away after Newtown, so for the past three weeks, in addition to the other work, we've been designing printable magazines."

"What kind of gun would something like this be used with? Are these for a rifle?"

"For both the AR and the AKM—the Kalashnikov."

"I see. And how much work have you done? Are these close to being usable?"

I watched the cars far behind me in the shop window's mirrored tinting.

"Well . . . I'm going out this weekend to test the first one. And we've made two others."

After we finished the call, I carried a smirk for the rest of the day.

When the engineer John met me at my apartment that Saturday, he offered to drive. I insisted on the honor and, after loading his machine gun in the back of the car, we staged at a gas station near South Congress and 290. After that it was south and to Lockhart, where the country opened up to a brief but stupendous emptiness. Once off the highway, we drove past an ashy, disintegrating church house. The empty bell tower briefly framed a patch of the gray clouds sagging overhead, which were torn like cotton batting.

Along a dirt road we followed a wire fence, the posts of which were old welding tanks beaten into the solid earth. The rust and paint at the tops of these had been baked by the sun into some kind of flaking ceramic. We drove over a cattle guard and were met as we kept on by a friendly pack of dogs.

"He's not here," John said of the owner of the place. He was still scanning ahead.

After rolling through a garden of shrapnel and machine parts, and at last a dogwood and a group of horses, we stopped beside a smaller fence that surrounded a sunken shooting gallery hemmed in by large clay berms.

We descended the easiest grade at the gallery and walked along an unlaid pipe resting beside a crusty ditch. The back of the gallery was lined with colored square targets and the iron profiles of birds and men. Alone out there, we pulled a pair of red, weathered tables together and set down the rifle case. I dragged some rusting metal chairs from around the gallery closer to us and we set to loading the first magazine, which crumpled and shattered after taking the first couple of brass cartridges.

We the let the pieces stay where they fell and worked with the second magazine I'd brought, this one thicker but still transparent, printed in PolyJet VeroClear. After loading ten rounds, John fired off a couple from his M16, a handsome colt with a short barrel and suppressor.

"What do you think?" I asked.

"Let's try automatic."

But the rifle kept spitting once and stopping. Yanking back the charging handle to eject the rounds, we found each punched and pinched. On the way out of the mag they would lodge on the metal feed ramps inside the upper receiver. The bolt would jam behind them.

"Looks like . . . ," John said, holding the rifle's ejection port up to the gray light. "Looks like the rounds are seated too low. Or that the lips on the mag are angled too sharply at their ends, maybe catching the back of the round as it comes out. Throwing the feed off."

I'd come to accept that things were going to break, that this trial-and-error period would inevitably mean failures along the way. But I don't think I was ever as zen and unsentimental as John, who, I was learning, took the unexpected and frustrating with near total equanimity. I supposed he had the dispassionate determination of a true engineer, the natural drive to see a problem and chew on it until he solved it. But he had to have pride, surely.

We spent the next couple of hours taking turns carving at the magazine. With nothing better on hand, we used our keys, making tiny white filings and turning in our rusty chairs to see in the last of the light. I remember thinking it was the most fun I'd had in months.

———

Early the next morning, I ran up to Liberty Hill to get a freshly printed magazine from Brian, which he had finished the night before. It would still have the flaws of those from the previous day's testing with John, but we'd meet again today to try to operate on it anyway. We could change the atoms if we couldn't change the bits. John stopped at my apartment around noon, and we sat on the floor with another of his black rifles, which I placed on a bath towel and propped up by its chunky bipod. I updated DD's Wiki Weapon development blog and left the door open for more light. John lay down to fit the magazine, charging the bolt to send unloaded rounds out of the gun and skittering around my floor. He told me he'd brought graphite.

Back at Lockhart it had rained. We trudged through the slop in the middle of the shooting gallery and on firmer islands rose as our feet turned to hooved, clay stalks.

The feed lips broke on the remaining mag, the one that John and I had tried to clean up with our keys the day before. We held the new magazine in the M16's well while we loaded the rifle from half assembly. Still having little luck firing, we were soon dumping graphite into the magazine bodies to help them feed better. John winced at the sight of the graphite in his aluminum rifle.

Henry Fountain at the *Times* was calling. I held up the phone to John and asked him, "You see that? Do you know who that is? Give me ten shots. We get ten shots on this camera and then it can fall apart and I won't give a damn."

Soon the rifle was spitting violently, its dread rattle hanging in the air and echoing through the bony limbs of the surrounding trees. When we took it out to examine it, the magazine body was slightly charred. I gave my phone to John to capture the next rounds I'd fire. I just hoped the gun would all hold together long enough.

"Okay."

"I'm going to shoot and then say, 'How's that national conversation going?'"

The rifle wanted to roll with its weight in my hands.

"So, I'm going to shoot it, turn, and hold it like this, say the bit and then finish with 'by Defense Distributed in Austin, Texas.' Yeah?"

"Got it. On your mark," John said.

We celebrated at the Chisholm Trail BBQ, standing in the serving line with goofy smiles and plastic trays. We had ribs and potato salad and sat right beside the ghastly wood paneling, which, evoking the old fish houses of my youth, offered the unexpected comforts of home.

"That's the thing about national conversations," I said with my mouth full. "Not everyone gets to talk. Hey, put the phone camera on me again."

"Okay," John said, smiling as he watched me through the screen.

"Okay, now ask me, 'How does it taste?'"

"So, how does it taste?"

"Tastes like Dianne Feinstein's lunch!"

On our quiet drive back, John spoke up.

"Eighty-five miles an hour. This is the highest speed limit in the United States."

"Hmm," I grunted, too busy with an email from Amir Taaki, who had invited me out to Bratislava, Slovakia. I had told him I'd be out of money with DD soon and would be coming to Europe to meet my only significant donor. Amir said I should make a few weeks of it and see his network as well.

I put the video of the magazine work with John online. "Download today," it read; *4chan* went nuts.

> You remember that commercial against pirated films you used to see on DVDs and in the theaters? You wouldn't download a car.

> No, you obviously would.

The *Infowars* headline was a classic:

BREAKING:

PRINTABLE AR 30-ROUND MAGAZINES NOW AVAILABLE FOR DOWNLOAD,

SERIOUSLY

Soon I found out that the chairman of the DCCC had added magazines to his proposed Wiki Weapon ban. Andy Greenberg called to ask what I thought of this while I was walking the uneven concrete panels that clad the tree roots near the car wash on Thirty-Second.

"Of course I love it. It's incredible and reactionary. He means to expand the Undetectable Firearms Act by conflating two issues: physical detectability and traceability—which is really about legal *observability*. What we can see versus what we can find.

"If anyone would bother to read the UFA, they'd see language in expectation of other detection techniques after the nineteen eighties. Beyond metal detectors. This guy is now talking about 'undetectable magazines,' and the gun community is throwing up its hands. What? The most popular commercial magazines are plastic. The only metal is the spring. But he's not an idiot. He can hide behind the security norm and use this bill to create gun control by other means."

Andy was listening politely but seemed less than interested in the finer point.

"I'm frustrated too," I told him. "Am I helping make this guy Steve Israel's career? I feel him back there on my coattails a little. And I'm thinking, 'Should I keep the next thing a secret?' I mean, he doesn't even have to work for it. There's this buffet approach. He'll just say 'Ooh, that too,' when we do a printed stock, or barrel or casing. It all makes you think about the time and resources a society spends just avoiding the consequences of its own technologies."

I later drove back down Highway 1 to spend my last time at J&B. I didn't ask them exactly why, but the boys evidently couldn't make the business work. Jackson had told me pretty suddenly, but maybe I should have known. Inside the shop, I climbed up a ladder against a makeshift carport and surveyed the pallet racks and the black floor. I walked on a steel beam and over a roll of chicken wire while I spoke down toward Jackson.

"I'd have liked to keep going here with you guys."

Jackson was moving toward the open garage door with two young men and a woman, the three impeccably styled. He looked up at me.

"You don't have to give it up, man. Could be all yours for six grand a month."

"Yeah. Thanks anyway." I laughed. But I'd lose my pending firearms license if I couldn't quickly find another lease.

Jackson walked outside with the trio.

As I came stepping back down a ladder, he returned to the office.

"Aw, hey, what the fuck," he said looking outside, from where he had come. He flung out his hands as a white diesel Rabbit scooted out of view.

"These fucking hipsters, man."

"What just happened?" I asked.

"Man, they paid for the car and I told them to wait while I went back to get the title. And they drive off! 'Cause they think its *so cool* not to have one."

He spat.

————

I drove the charred magazine and printed rifle parts to Dallas for a meeting with Glenn Beck. Past the city of Temple I saw a billboard for the Apocalypse:

August2nd2027.com On the Mount of Olives at Noon!

Haroon had called me with an important update. The DEF-CAD server logs were full of visits from every authority in the country. Department of Homeland Security. Department of Justice. NASA. NY.gov.

The heat was around the corner, surely. But what do you do?

Maybe I should have prepared for the interview, but all I could think about during my drive was Nancy Lanza. In the weeks after Sandy Hook there was this fascinating secondary narrative in the press. Of course there was every kind of attempt to associate the family with ideology or the Tea Party. But the aftermath was producing an unstated consensus that, regardless, the atrocity was squarely the mother's fault.

It started with bad parenting. She should have reached out for help sooner, and maybe she was delusional and too accommodating, unable to see her son's increasing instability. The conservatives and NRA types did rearguard work for the more explicit consensus that clinical and systemic failures of oversight contributed directly to the tragedy. To prevent other incidents like this, we should strengthen mental health screening, turn doctors and nurses into agents of the court, etc. But beneath the louder consensus was something much more subtle: Nancy Lanza's consignment to political purgatory.

Did it begin with the discovery that, when she broke up her family unit, she had turned to arms instead of federal support? Instead of getting remarried to Uncle Sam, had this divorcée sacrificed something in attempting a life of independence and embracing the poisonous gun culture? Was her ultimate sin sharing this forbidden knowledge with her son? And what knowledge was that, specifically? That protection is available outside the state? Was her fate the just deserts of those who stay out partying too late and take to the sword? A curious reversal of the usually lauded "empowered single mother."

I recalled the recent statements of the Teleprompted:

> If there is even one thing we can do to reduce this violence, if there's even one life that can be saved, we've got an obligation to try.

A fine doctrinal distillation: life reduced to the simultaneous purpose and aim of politics. "If we can save just one." The slogan of popular administration and the motto of the Bare Life Movement. But he who determines a value also fixes a nonvalue.

The city leaders affixed twenty-six stars to the Newtown firehouse. Campaigns on Facebook called for people to commit twenty-six acts of kindness, while we should light twenty-six candles at memorials. The Teleprompted himself would eulogize "those twenty beautiful children and six teachers." But twenty-seven people had been executed on December 14, 2012. Between the waves of benediction and righteous recommitment, Nancy Lanza had imperceptibly passed over a threshold.

Perhaps she was a wayward excessive, a true accomplice to her son's crime, or a zealot who put her faith in false metal idols. Maybe this really was a modern Medea whose politics threatened to render vengeance upon us all. But she had certainly passed the limit beyond which her life was politically relevant. Her death was not a murder.

North of Dallas I exited to drift past newly minted suburban developments and toward a giant studio lot. I walked the paved incline to a brick plaza and the glass portico of the leftmost building. It was as large as an aircraft hangar. I stood at the doorway and buzzed the desk there, telling the guard I had some things to bring in. To my right, against another building's side, an enormous mural spanned the wall. A cartoon family watched me from the balcony of a painted arcade.

Minutes later I walked back toward the portico with my ghostly wares wrapped loosely in a vinyl sheet. A man and a woman wearing plastic badges were leaving from the opposite direction. My rifle barrel saluted them as they passed, and I saw them eye it with silent anxiety.

PART VIII

Modern Politics

I landed in Vienna under a sky of solid white. Past arrivals, I hit the ATM and settled into a plastic swivel chair to enjoy the continental elegance of the airport McCafé, waiting for my SIP service to work. I fiddled with the phone and ran through a battery of other apps, noticing the cold at my heels, which slipped in from the constant yawn of the double sets of doors to the outside. In a half hour I caved and bought a T-Mobile data plan. I shot an email and some texts over to Mike Gogulski, who had been boarding Amir at his place for the past month, just over the Austrian border in Bratislava, Slovakia. He'd be my host for the first leg of my European fund-raising tour.

What bus do I take again?

You want Novy Most. Let me know what time you leave and I'll meet you there.

I exited through the sliding doors and walked into a rush of cold. Stepping between a line of buses and to an outer drive, I dropped my bags at a concrete bench and took in the plastic bus schedule posted there. A handful of buses came and went, each making boiling noises and taking a huddled group in from the freeze. By the time I began to shiver, I found a ride for Bratislava. I didn't know a thing about Mike personally. I had seen him on Amir's mailing list, the "system undo crew," assumed he was young like me, and I read about his work organizing the Free Bradley Manning campaign in the early days after the leaks. I read he had given up his American citizenship voluntarily, forgoing picking up any other. He was known then for being one of the world's few intentionally "stateless" persons.

On the bus ride I looked out over the winter fields and the stretching snowbanks. The fence line dissolved into and peeked out again from the white. I leaned against the cold window and watched anxiously past the driver and down the coming road. We approached the river and a suspension bridge with some clamshell building atop a spire. Out through the fog I saw concrete-panel high-rises overwhelming the hillside, the gaunt ruins of some brutal utopia. The whole place had been shelled by the sixties and the Communist era, and looked untouched by any Velvet Revolution.

I left the bus under the dripping river bridge and danced between a mound of slush. Most of the group queued at the side while the driver ran around to pull luggage from the undercarriage. I looked past them and began walking toward a ticket stand. A husky man in glasses, a black cloak and a knit cap approached me, presumably Mike. His face was red in the cold and his stubble gray. He nodded and made his way to me.

"Cody."

I pulled at the strap of my pack and shook his gloved hand.

"Any other bags?"

I looked down reflexively to check my orange duffel. I shook my head.

"Let's go, then."

As we walked I looked up toward a hill and in the gray brilliance saw a castle. Mike and I passed from under the highway bridge to an older quarter. Where there wasn't snow, I slipped as we went.

"You might have wanted different shoes."

We entered an iced-over square and trudged between a pair of narrow, barren fountains. A pointless channel, as far as I could tell. Mike stopped and for a second waited. As I stepped beside him, he pointed to a building whose annex adjoined the square.

"That's the embassy."

From the black SUVs at the curb, I supposed I knew the one he meant.

"Around oh-nine—yeah, I think it was oh-nine—they did this project to improve the security of the building. Where previously there was a small chain-link fence"—his finger traced a line I couldn't follow—"they added a mega fence and that checkpoint box you see sticking out." He smiled. "I call it the man trap."

"Looks like something from City Seventeen," I added.

"They expanded the fenced-off area," he went on, still pointing.

It occurred to me that we were alone and in the open, so I supposed I wasn't the only one for whom he intended his presentation.

"Added those stone posts there. They even incorporated the statue of Pavol Hviezdoslav as a security feature. A nice obstacle for the perimeter barrier. Pretty sweet, right?" His tone was mordant, nearly caustic.

I didn't speak. I later read about Hviezdoslav, the Slovak poet, dramatist, and writer. During the darkest days of Hungarian repression in the region, he was part of a group who kept Slovak literature alive in spite of censorship and persecution. Their organization, Slovak Matica, was shut down and its property confiscated before it was reopened in 1919 when Czechoslovakia was first founded. Mike wanted me to see how callously the US government had incorporated a people's symbol into their security perimeter.

"Do you see at all the birdhouses in the trees here? Look."

"What about them?"

"Don't speak too loud around them."

Mike walked on with his hands in his pockets, and I followed him into a diner at the square's edge. We were seated at a sad little table, and I stared at the green baseboards before we ordered tiny bits of breakfast meats. He asked if I was tired. We talked there for a bit, and even the silences were friendly.

Afterward we walked past the National Theater and along a row of shops. I looked down at my phone as we took another corner and came to a street named Groslingnova.

"Oh, are you getting maps out here?" Mike asked.

I eyed the dead gray icon amid the empty blur on the screen.

"Supposed to be . . ."

"Amir has both of my spares right now, so ask him for the key when we get up there."

We passed between the cars at the curb, all caked in white. Through a café window I could see a small crowd dining against oil-colored wallpaper.

"Shit," Mike said, squinting as he reached for the door. "One of my minders in there. Just let me talk."

As we walked inside, the girl behind the bar greeted Mike. I glanced at the pastry trays and the espresso machine and could hardly see her over the glassed-in dessert cooler. Mike only nodded to the girl as he turned his attention to the gentleman in the corner near the window, who rose as he saw us. He was tall and wore a black T-shirt and light-washed jeans in a cut from the turn of the century. Wearing a black cap, he smiled and spoke in a casual, wholly American accent:

"Mike, I'm so happy to see you again." And without diverting his look or expression he added, "And who is this you've brought with you today?"

I glanced quickly at Mike, who seemed to counsel reservation.

"My name is Cody."

"Cody, we haven't seen you around here before. From Texas, I see?"

My grip tightened around the straps of my Longhorn duffel bag. I chanced a pause to let Mike pick up the conversation. As he did, the tall man's head swiveled back to him. I began to stare at his fixed smile.

"He's visiting for a bit," Mike said. "For a little conference we've put together."

Mike moved around the bar as he spoke. I stepped alongside.

"I'm sure I'll see you two later!" the tall man yelled, still standing.

We hit a dark panel door that opened to a concrete hallway, which sent a plunging echo everywhere about us.

"What the hell was that?" I hissed at Mike, the sound of my flustered question traveling along the naked walls.

"Hey, like I said."

I had no idea if he was joking about having a minder. I searched his face to see that he was surely, surely putting me on.

As we stepped into the yellow cage elevator, I was furious. But whether it was at Mike for springing that interaction on me, or at myself for having no idea how to live in this new world I had chosen, I couldn't say. As we rose in the creaking box, I heard the lights shut out in the hall below us with a *chunk*. At Mike's floor, we squeezed around a sliding door to a broken balcony lined with bird spikes.

Amir saw me when at last we entered, and threw out his arms to give me a hug.

"Come, come. I want you to meet Mihai."

I shook the hand of a tall young man, as pale as I, with dark-black hair. As he smiled, he kept his eyes nearly closed under his heavy brow. Amir spoke enthusiastically about the bloodstain on his hoodie and delayed no further in giving it a full presentation. He and his boys had defended a squat in London near Pimlico against the police at the end of the year. One of the Queen's properties.

"And these fucking fascists. One of these cops was scum. I told him to his face. I told him he was a fascist and he chose to work for fascists. To beat the people instead of work for them."

"What did he say?" I asked Amir.

"Aw, he says, 'I'm proud of my job and at least *I* work. I feed my family.'"

Amir puffed out his chest and swung his arms.

"'I don't take from society like you lot,'" he said, continuing his impersonation. "And what have I taken from you? Just what was it that I took?"

"Oh, by the way . . . ," Mike began.

Amir's energy muted what Mike had to say: "Everyone seems to have gotten the flu in the last few days. I think Mihai still has it. Thought you should know."

Mihai nodded absently as he walked back to the end of a long couch across from Mike's bed, to which Mike now moved to sit. I sat down beside Amir, who began explaining the guest list for his miniature Bitcoin conference to be held in a few days' time. I unpacked my bags and for a while thereafter I watched him sketch in his journal.

That night I didn't sleep. In the early hours Mike whispered to me so as to not alert Mihai and Amir, who were now sleeping in the other room.

"Hey."

I looked over from the couch to where Mike sat up in his bed, draped in a sheet like an ancient magistrate, all golden in the lamplight. I moved closer to better hear him.

"I know you're here to fund-raise and be shown around by Amir. But he's going to try to introduce you to Sasha, and I just want you to be careful of that guy."

"Okay, well, who is Sasha? Why should I be worried?"

"The best way I can say it is that he's one of these exiled Russian oligarchs. If you are even remotely a threat to Putin, from wealth or political popularity, you don't stay in Russia too long.

All I know is this guy has a lot of business concerns around Europe and he used to be in government. And now he's *here*." Mike leaned toward me then.

"Well, he's helping Amir, right?" I asked. "Doesn't that mean he's friendly to us? To our politics, even?"

Mike dismissed this quickly. "Amir is too trusting and we all know it. He's not being careful, so I want you to hear it from me because you're not going to hear it from him. Just watch out. Getting involved with these people isn't a game."

Two days later I was sick. Oblivious to my souring mood and diminishing health, Amir invited me out to a restaurant that night. I had a hard time making sense of our route given the dark and the headlights skating over the street corners, which were buried in ice. Along the way we talked about fund-raising and how we got by with our projects.

"Where is your guy, again?" Amir asked. The cars came over the hills. "You said you already had a patron."

"Switzerland," I said. "I don't really know what to expect when I go, but he knows I'm here now." Back in the first weeks, an industrialist had started funding our efforts. As part of the deal, he asked that we keep his identity a secret, and I'd never had a reason to not comply with the request.

"Even if that doesn't work out, you can work with Sasha, I bet."

"Yeah? Tell me about him. What's the story there, again?"

In the Old Town we took a back stairway to a bustling hall lined with benches. The menu was in Slovak. When the waitress came to take our order, I held out my hand, deferring to Amir, sure he was more comfortable in the language.

"We want *meat*," he slowly mouthed. "*Not spi-cee.*" He shook his head and pointed to his gnashing teeth.

I jerked unconsciously and looked up at the waitress, who stared at me blankly until I nodded and she walked away. I wondered what all that would bring us.

"It's getting hard to reach the kids, man," Amir started. "All they want to do is, I don't know, talk about Harry Potter or something." He pronounced the last word *some-fing*, and I wondered if his working-class accent was a bit exaggerated.

"If I could do that speech in London over," I told Amir, "I'd make it about mythologizing the roles of institutions in our lives. That's what Harry Potter is to me. Expert knowledge as the ordering of the world. The university discourse at war with the dark magic of sectarianism. It's no coincidence at all that freshman convocation scene is filmed in the Harvard cafeteria.

"Muahahaha!" Amir laughed and threw his head back.

"And it's typical, post-heroic Englishness. Our superheroes still go into compliance when they graduate."

We went on like that for a while longer until our food arrived. *Meat*. Not spicy and in a sauce with noodles as slick as the phlegm in my throat.

After we'd both set our utensils down, I probed him about working together.

"Yeah, yeah. There will be time for that," Amir said. "There's so many other things I want to tell you about first!"

When the check came, and he made no move for it, I began to suspect my friend's hospitality would be most often my own.

I asked Mike how to not get water absolutely everywhere when using his shower.

"Yeah . . . the Europeans still haven't figured out the whole shower thing yet."

I began to work and sleep on the yellowed couch in the kitchenette, receiving nightly visits from Mike's cat Charlie, who preferred to walk over me on his way to the windowsill.

My pending federal firearms license application was in trouble. Unable to find a replacement lease in Austin, I had convinced Daniel Fisher to let me use his address out in Fredericksburg until I could get another prospect. I wanted to find another spot in town, but they were few and far between—well, places for rent on a student's budget, anyway. But Daniel had emailed after I was abroad to say he just couldn't keep his end of the deal. Too much was at risk, and he didn't want to jeopardize his relationship with his landlord.

John, my new engineer friend, had been emailing as well since I'd left. He wanted to take on a larger role with the project than just helping with magazines. He'd even queried me about adding a new printer to our rotation. I asked him to first just give me time to find a place for our FFL while I was gone. The ATF had given me until early February. In another week I'd relent and ask John to rent me a tiny space in his father's warehouse on Regal Row, at the very edge of Austin. I had no idea then how comically cramped the space would be.

In the mornings the divide between Mike's flat and the one behind sounded like a concrete canyon. All was quiet but for the shout of a dumpster door closing and echoing up the walls. Then the plastic wheels would take the grit and resound through the backstreet. I stepped over Mike's cat when I got up, taking my stiffened clothes from a flimsy drying rack. Walking by a dresser, I'd often spot a few iridescent Casascius coins, the well-crafted physical form of our dear bitcoin.

One morning, when I opened the miniature refrigerator, I saw two empty bottles.

"Uh, Mike, we're out of tonic water." That was the only thing any of us were drinking.

Mike groaned something inaudible from around the threshold.

"You want me to get some more? I was thinking of getting some socks anyway."

I closed the little door and went for my thin coat and then, shivering and febrile, made my way to the shops.

On the day Amir took me to meet Sasha, I had almost forgotten to be apprehensive. Leaving a snow-swept alley, Amir and I passed by a blue church in the Secession style. At Stone Square I took in the enormous and abandoned Hotel Kyjev. We walked through the Old Town and back to the bus stop under the river bridge. The rain came in drips and then bursts with the passing of the heavier vehicles overhead. A massive pier was covered in the graffiti caricature of some Soviet partisan. He was fat and unshaven in his military dress.

"I know you're excited," Amir said. "We're going to get you some funds today!"

I appreciated his enthusiasm. It would cost DD a couple thousand just getting in and out of Europe. And I'd been doing little more than getting by while I was here. DD's materials budget was

still okay for continuing with magazines and receivers, but I figured I needed another ten grand or so to acquire our own FDM
machine and bankroll another four or five months of runway. It
would be nice to have legal defense money in case the DOJ started
poking around.

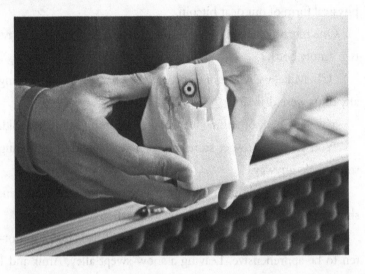

We took the bus to Vienna. Passing alongside an old border
village, Amir brought up the European Central Bank's new report
on Bitcoin, which at that time had simply mentioned the prospect
of regulation.

"Everyone says it could have been worse!" he exclaimed. "This
is the consensus. But these are the same people who accept the
'being moderate' fallacy. Like if there are two factions, they will
balance out and the market will somehow find the best solution,
despite being rigged by the powerful using influence and power to
establish their vise grip on Bitcoin."

I nodded. I said the American gun industry was already long in
the hands of the state, making it very hard to do anything innova-

tive as a private person. Both sides, the manufacturers and the political class, even preferred it that way. It would be terrible if bitcoiners were to just sleepwalk into letting the bureaucrats license their firms and activities.

"There's this bitcoin honey badger meme now which really gets under my skin," Amir went on. "In essence it goes that it doesn't matter what people or governments do, Bitcoin can just shrug it off and keep going. But it's this simplistic lens, you know. It discards all of the technological issues and threats facing the protocol that we strive to protect against. Even people like Andreas push this. The idea is that Bitcoin as a consensus system subject to all power groups acting on it is an invincible agent of change no matter what. That it will infect the system and deploy a takeover. And so . . . driven by this view, there is this overwhelming push for 'the mainstream,' and in part you can see this is incentivized by the price. But there's this push that at all costs, *we must achieve the mainstream*."

"They don't realize the importance of their own human network," I submitted. "They've overestimated the technology at the expense of their values and philosophy. They'll lose their grip on both."

"In the Esperanto movement, there was a split between two camps. *Fina Venko* means Final Victory. They taught about some future event where Esperanto would reach that vital tipping point, at which point the dam would burst and Esperanto would become the dominant language around the globe. The Raumistoj rejected the Fina Venko. They instead taught that the real value of Esperanto is its culture, as a movement and as a language. They reject the Final Victory as a distraction and a dangerous illusion. I reject the Fina Venko of Bitcoin."

In downtown Vienna we listened to the splattering on the pavement. We walked on as the ice fell in chunks from the roof-tops and busted before and behind us in the street. The sun was out between the rows of maisonettes, and the melt ran in cords from the dripstones. We came to a wrought-iron cage against a door in the middle of an apartment block and buzzed in.

After a moment spent securing our bags, we entered an unlit art deco lobby and took a marbled, helical stair. The very top was cold and cavernous. Amir knocked on the heavy door and we waited, and there was Sasha's lieutenant to let us in.

"Will it be just you two?"

"Yes," Amir answered.

We walked two or three steps down a simple hallway with black, polished floors. A middle-aged woman turned around a corner near an office. The blond lieutenant led us into a kitchen-ette where Sasha stood deliberating with another man. *Short* wasn't the right word for his stature. Maybe *compact*. But he stood with an incredible bearing and with his shaved head looked fight-ing fit. He moved deliberately in cotton slippers and spoke softly, welcoming us. Amir spoke first.

"Sasha, this is Cody."

"I am familiar with him," said Sasha. "One of the most dan-gerous men in the world?" His expression didn't change as he stepped around his black marble bar, but his lieutenant smiled.

Ah, *that*. This moment wouldn't be the last time I'd wished the journalists at *Wired* understood what they were doing lobbing that title at me. The real Billy Badasses of the world took it as a challenge.

Sasha looked me in the eye, and I didn't have anything to say.

"Are you in from Texas? Will you stay much longer?"

"I'll be following Amir for a time," I replied. "I was hoping you and I might discuss what I'm doing with my company."

"Well, you are welcome here," said Sasha. "Will you gentlemen need the password for the wireless? Damon, please find Julia. We will need the password."

Sasha made us tea and spoke to us more with this uniquely gentle and quiet certainty. His English was not heavily accented.

"I hope we can do some planning here today, Amir. I need a commitment from you as well. Is this really the space you want? And can you fill it?"

It had been totally unclear to me until now, but Sasha had agreed to purchase the location for Amir's next Bitcoin conference. Amir had gone on about his plans for it but would talk about it only abstractly or in details completely out of any locatable context. He told Sasha he wanted the UN building in Vienna. They argued about the scope of the event, and after a while we were dismissed. Sasha told us to return another day.

On the way to the bus stop, I asked Amir if he would like to stop at a café. He instead pulled me into a grocery and piled prosciutto and a baguette in my arms.

"Do we want anything else?" I asked, moving toward the checkout, which seemed comically long for so small a shop.

"Apples! We should get apples!" Amir ran back into the aisles as I waited.

To eat, we wandered into the public part of a street-side bank. It would be closing soon. A professional-looking woman came in from the street and filled out a tiny paper slip at an island counter. She regarded us nervously as Amir ate and drew on his corduroy pants with a felt-tipped pen he had managed to produce from no-where at all. We sat in the corners of the bank window like dirty mannequins, watching the light desert the sky and the snow turn orange under the streetlamps. In another hour, we slowly crossed the road back to the crusty bus stop.

———

John had been regularly sending me updates while I was away, using TrueCrypt volumes to keep our correspondence safe from prying eyes. The most recent of these was about the new FDM printer. He had found a Stratasys Dimension SST on eBay, but the shippers had dented it with their forklift and then pretended nothing had happened to it when he came to pick it up.

Tonight, distracted by the dried spittle from days of coughing and sneezing on my screen, I read a more amusing update:

> I brought in an intern from work. After I explained what
> our team already knew about Stratasys printers, he figured
> out Stratasys's encryption algorithm within an hour. The
> machine is simply a Linux box with poorly implemented
> security. They attempted to encrypt the cartridge material
> level using EEPROMs on each cartridge that have
> permanently burned serial numbers. However, they
> pass their encryption key in plain text to a built-in Linux
> decryption block and even left a debug commenting
> present saying so ;). There's also no limit on how 'full'
> a cartridge can be . . . 12043%? Sure! Never run out of
> plastic again ;)

I wondered if I should post the news to our development blog. Perhaps I'd wait until I had a bigger audience. John went on.

> I attached the ATF Form you requested. It's three pages
> long. Note the third page is just a paperwork reduction
> act notice!

Amir asked that we all go out when his Berliner friends got to Bratislava. Other radicals in town joined us for a meet-up he'd organized. What gathered later in that basement bar may have been one of the rudest squads of world-eaters and blackguards to meet in Europe in a half century. System hardeners, privacy extremists, and programmers helping to launder the money for Europe's best crime families. Mihai entertained us with his idea for a peer-to-peer marketplace he called *egora*. Amir shouted his mottos and squealed with laughter. I took a liking to the grousing Mormon across from me who was bemused by his own animal lust for the waitress and each pretty young thing to walk in that night. I suppose we were each of us bastards. A gang destined for Hull, Halifax, or Hell.

At one point they asked me about the gun debate back home. And I said it was all about "gun sense" now. The prohibitionists had gone underground to focus-group a new middle-class vocabulary of products liability and safety. Focus-grouped to hell, I said. Every gun use was coded as part of a singular "public health problem," one worked on by Diane Sawyer and the like. The professional left was producing a new biology for Johnny Public. *What made you feel you needed to buy a gun, sir? Do you have any anger issues you'd like to talk about? There's a 'script for that.* The subject now medicalized, they were free to develop the pathologies of gun ownership. The bad faith of the Bare Life Movement. Throw the gun owner into the woodchipper of the academic interpretive machinery.

I turned to my Mormon friend. "Like the one in Salt Lake, funding digs in Central America for Lamanite skulls; you could say there's a crystal cathedral at work."

He smiled dimly, then groaned as I went on.

"Of course it doesn't matter if there are actual pathologies related to gun ownership. The point is in the production. Produce an artificial norm against which a politically problematic division of the population can be measured and categorized. Turn them into objects of administrative power.

I held up my hands. "This is modern politics."

"You should be on the liquid cosh," I then recalled a nasty Brit had told me by email. Clearly I was a danger to Western sociality, but the good man still respected my absolute right to keep existing as a drugged piece of meat. At least I still deserved the treatment of an animal or the criminally insane. Human rights, in other words. But of course this is one of the first avenues back to the logic of the camps. An agonist once put it this way: "If man was once a being whose question was political, today his politics brought into question his being."

By now I'd learned I'd rather my enemies just have the nerve to want me dead.

At the end of the week I explored Bratislava's Old City alone. By night I followed what was left of the ruined city wall around a hill to St. Michael's Gate, traveling behind a man and his little white dog. I listened to the tiny slaps of its paws echo through the alley in the dark.

PART IX

Dropping the Liberator

Mihai and I set out for Amir's gathering at the hackerspace Progressbar. I stayed a step behind him, watching my Romanian friend navigate the cobbled streets and cramped corners. I had told Ben by email that Mihai read Falkvinge, the first leader of the Pirate Party. Among his other responsibilities, Mihai was the editor-in-chief of *Bitcoin* magazine, a position I was told he took after an employee of the magazine ran off with 200,000 bitcoin. Serious money, even at the start of 2013.

We slipped through a breezeway and into the stark wind. We passed a gate and climbed a marbled spiral stair. At the highest floor, from behind the first door, I heard a great murmur. Inside were freaks and gangsters, dissidents and hackers, madmen and millionaires. All wrapped in dull coats and scarves, you wouldn't have been able to tell the geniuses from the criminals. But then, that's a false choice. They all sat on top of each other on broken chairs and couches, many leaning against the drab sea-green walls or standing like spooks in the back.

When we squeezed through the door, Peter Šurda, who was quickly being recognized as Bitcoin's first dedicated economist, was presenting a preview of his master's thesis. He had projected graphs on the wall showing the last year of transaction volume at Mt. Gox, the world's largest bitcoin exchange. I saw peaks and troughs, but didn't take much more from it than that. A pair of hackers to my left were whispering about the recent collapse of Bitcoinica, and how it had tarnished Amir. I sat beside Mihai with my legs crossed against the back wall, double-cloaked and on edge, and trying not to cough.

Amir fooled with the projector, and the audience shouted as Peter concluded and fell back into the crowd. Amir flicked his laptop to the *Wiki Weapon* development blog, and in a blink an image of Daniel Fisher with his black rifle colored the wall.

The din shrank noticeably.

"Where is Cody? Can someone find Cody?" Amir yelled into the semidark and brushed his hood back to squint.

I stood and took a step, sniffling. Amir bobbed his head with glee and slapped my coated shoulder as he sat back down with the crowd. Turning to my left, I began.

"My name is Cody Wilson and the group is Defense Distributed. If you know about us, it's because of the Wiki Weapon, our effort to use current 3D printers—what's available today—to try to print a handgun that can use common and available ammunition. But of course it's not enough to print it. Wiki Weapon is about releasing the software for the gun with an open-source license so that anyone the world over can download and make it."

I began motioning for Amir to scroll through the pictures on the blog.

"The effort is working so well because it confuses the stakes for free-speech liberals and command-and-control liberals. The files themselves are a powerful species of political speech. And how do we know they are political speech?"

I looked to the back.

"Because they're being fought so strongly."

I turned back to the wall and raised my hand to the washed-out images of rifle receivers there. I reminded Amir that there was a YouTube video to play as well.

"At the end of last year we began printing rifle receivers for the AR-15. These would break at four or five rounds. We made changes in software and printed in different materials. This"—I pointed to the next images—"is the same family of receiver in January."

The video of Daniel and Tyler in their war gear firing dozens of rounds in rapid fire screamed through the tinny computer speakers beside a ratty love seat. I watched the room and all the quiet looks.

"Just before I got here, we started working on rifle magazines. I hadn't expected it—really, it makes sense—but these are even easier to make. Perfect for the current materials."

I signaled Amir to speed up the scrolling.

"After studying these materials and building out a team, I believe we can have a handgun within two months."

I looked back up to the projected image of a blog post I had made about the chairman of the DCCC.

"We are doing this in the face of the most intense opposition private semiautomatic ownership has had in the US in a generation. And what's more . . . we're winning. Thank you."

I swelled with the room's applause.

"Would anyone like to ask Cody a question?" Amir asked.

One came from a man seated on a couch near the window. He looked to someone on his left and then leaned forward, speaking casually.

"Are you proud of what you've done?"

I didn't say anything for a moment. "Look, you just heard my fucking presentation. So what? You're better than me? You can moralize to me?"

His face reddened and the room was silent.

"How about I print you a fucking boot to lick?"

I coughed into my closed fist. "Are there any other questions?"

No one spoke up.

"Great."

The crowd parted as I stepped back to the room's rear, where Mihai stood, eyes wide.

When the event had ended, Sasha approached me, flanked by his scarved entourage. He gingerly put on his leather gloves.

"Cody, Amir will be visiting tomorrow. Will you be coming as well?"

I told him he would see me there.

After our event, the stairwell took the throngs of young men and echoed their talk of heading for the bars. I invited Mihai a few blocks over to a basement kitchen. We descended quickly, before anyone could ask to join us.

We took a street near St. Michael's to a back alley, and turned to enter a basement tavern. There we were surrounded by candle-light and glass. We were seated at a small table, and Mihai leaned against the stonework.

"Almost a year ago my father had a stroke," Mihai told me, after we'd discussed the conference. "Not much longer after that, he had a second stroke on the same cerebral hemisphere. At first I'm thinking, you know, I am devastated, and I think with horror he will remain as a vegetable. And this time it's over. After the first stroke he recovered quite well, I would say seventy to eighty percent. The only issue remaining was his fluency. He required more time sometimes to find the words."

Mihai paused for a moment and his eyes narrowed as his expression darkened. "After the second stroke, and the discharge from neurology, he could hardly speak, and his right hand could not move at all. He had trouble moving his foot. Two weeks after coming home, he was referred to a physiotherapy hospital that I didn't know about. It was a strange building in an old mansion. I didn't know it existed."

Mihai's hands sat inert on the table, splayed with his thumbs pointing to the side as if he was forming a leaky cup with them.

"My first reaction was insult, you know. I was trying to save my father, and this place did not look like a hospital. I was not impressed. But the next day, when I went to visit my father, I was so surprised. He had begun to move his right hand—a hand he had not moved for over a month. He began to make amazing progress that reminded me of the days after his release from his first admission. He began to walk with a crutch and he began to speak. And I can see the improvements are because of the great staff here, that this is the best physiotherapy in the whole city."

Mihai's face brightened briefly and then fell back into shadow.

"So, the hospital manager, maybe you would say director, from some wisdom I learn has decided to close this beautiful place with forty beds. They said it was expenses. So, I think, I can do something about this. I can help and make the difference. I started a social media campaign, and I wrote letters and sent emails to high officials. We rallied the people and—I did not expect this—after all this the hospital at last said it would stay!"

Mihai's eyes clouded over. He sipped his drink, and then, as he resumed his story, his voice grew increasingly faint. "Visiting my father after this, I feel like a hero, you know. The nurse says the manager wants to see me in his office. I think, and I am humble about it, but I think I am about to be praised. Maybe offered some reward or recognition. The manager asks me to sit in the chair. And he is very curt. I am thinking, This is strange.

"The manager had his hands together and is shaking. His face is red. He tells me, 'Do you understand what you have done? This hospital was part of an arrangement far bigger than you and me. There are very bad and powerful people who depended on this building selling. Can you understand what you have done to my life?' "

We finished our drinks in silence.

Later, we left the tavern to the icy night. Along an open street gallery we came to a modest serving window. A burly old man in a paper hat leaned over his grill and looked up at us.

"Amir told me about this place," said Mihai.

We ordered two burgers. Standing in the new-fallen snow, we watched the weathered man work his great arms with an inexplicable deftness. The moon above was a mismounted scope, sighted on some outer heaven.

———————

Amir asked me to follow him to the train station. In less than two weeks I had resigned myself to being his miserable aide-de-camp. The Roger Rabbit to his Baby Herman. Wherever we'd travel, I'd be there to learn the trains, have the cash, defuse the tension. Along the way today we talked about Intersango, a bitcoin exchange he ran with his friend Patrick, the first such exchange in the UK. Diligent and true, they kept running the business until the very last bank had blacklisted them. With his light-blue hood cinched tight, Amir ran his hands along the bars of an iron fence.

"Sometimes it's just important to agitate," he said. "To piss on the roses."

We were joined at the station by Amir's sister and a couple of collaborators. We took the train to Vienna. As we waited for Sasha or one of his deputies outside the conference center at the UN building, I watched the crane tops above and around us dissolve in the lowering sky. Impatient, we broke in from the lobby. Alone in the main hall, Amir threw his arms wide and imagined aloud the spots for each group and table placement for his future Bitcoin conference.

"And here we'll have a village infrastructure."

A few suited people, sometimes alone and sometimes in groups, would pause at a balcony above us and eye us warily before turning around and disappearing.

Sasha never showed.

Our group took the underground to Sasha's office. His lieutenants asked us to wait in an anteroom while he conferenced with a software developer. "All right," he said, upon appearing from behind the double doors a half hour later.

"It's time for you all to leave. Cody, you and Amir will stay."

We waited alone, as Sasha returned to his conference room.

After another twenty minutes, at last a lieutenant returned to us. "He wants you to come back later tonight. Ten."

Amir took us to a Vienna hackerspace to kill time, and I soon fell asleep on a couch in a back room. When I woke, I was looking up at some great bearded programmer with a cigarette hanging from his mouth.

"Where is Amir?" I asked.

He finished exhaling smoke with a purse of his lips. "Who is Amir?"

Slumped and unmoving on the ratty couch, I looked over slowly to watch some hollow-cheeked curiosity hunched over his keyboard playing *Minecraft*. The blue light blanked the lenses in his glasses and his mouth was agape.

"What do you do?"

My eyes traveled back to the moldering Teuton.

"You know 3D printing?"

"Mmm." He blew smoke.

"I'm the guy printing the gun."

He nodded, tapped his cigarette on a glass tray, and said something in German to the boy digging in the digital sandbox.

"Yes, I have seen it. You. Quite exciting," he said.

I raised my right arm to cock my thumb and point. "Bang."

When I woke again, Amir had still not returned. I leaned over and off the couch and stretched my arm for the door. I left the dank closet and came directly into a classroom, class in session. Each student was at his desk facing a projection screen. I walked crouching beneath the burst from the rear projector and under the line of sight of a large swiveling television camera. I kept my back against the wall until I turned down a cinder-block corridor.

In a tiny wooden room sat an odd council. I found Amir at the head of the table.

"Ah, we were just talking about you, Cody. This is Eric, a professor at the university."

I gave Eric and the others at the table a weak acknowledgment.

"It's time to get out of here, Amir."

When we came back through the classroom, Amir grabbed the TV camera, mock-moving it toward me while addressing the cameraman.

"You should film this, man. Don't you know what this man is doing?"

When we got back to Sasha's, a different agent greeted us. I had not seen him before. Sasha directed the two of us to wait in his little conference room. As we waited, Amir showed me an email from one his contacts, a Chinese national. He was begging to invest in something, anything, of Amir's.

"Do you have any ideas for him?"

"Nothing besides a lending or anonymity idea. But Amir, we really need to get that dumb money in China. I mean, forget the startup stuff, think geopolitically. A partial Chinese state embrace of bitcoin is a serious challenge to the dollar. This is playing the game at a high level."

Amir's eyes sparkled.

Sasha came in and spoke softly. "Amir, it's time for you to go to the other room."

And with that, Amir dutifully gathered his notebooks and quickly stepped out the double doors. His élan bewildered me. Was it literally going to get me killed?

Sasha directed his lieutenant to sit to our right.

"I saw your presentation, Cody. Are you trying to commercialize any aspect of this?"

I told him that I wasn't and that though I'd been on the lookout along the way, I didn't see too many ways to do so.

His lieutenant spoke up. "What about a toy? You get children and their parents to log on to design a custom toy gun."

I was sure it was attractive, I said, but no, that's not really what I was about. Sasha nodded and turned to the wall.

"Can you make this?"

Projected on the screen was a black rifle with a thick, suppressed barrel. It had a skeletonized stock and looked very, very Russian. I told them the technology I was using was only polymer, but an Austrian firm named Lithoz had recently commercialized a ceramic sintering process that might get something like this done. We went on like that a little longer. They wrote it all down.

"Amir"—Sasha was still directing us as we put on our coats and scarves to leave—"go and stay at Gregory's house tonight. He will send you the number."

We walked an hour or better to a stylish apartment. Gregory was at home with his girlfriend. He praised our intrepidness and his boss. He told us what it was like to fly Gaddafi from Africa.

"How did you meet your girlfriend?" I asked.

"It was at a concert," she said, answering for him and smiling.

"I hope you'll pardon me but there's this thing I've noticed about the girls back in Bratislava," I said to her. "Is it this way to you? They are so pretty but their faces are sad. Like they're already much older than their years."

Everyone nodded in silence at the table.

Soon I was washing my feet in the bathtub, tossing my ratty socks in the trash can there. I could overhear the lieutenant talking with Amir.

"Maybe your friend is smart, but tell him to stop making guns, Amir. No one in Europe likes guns."

That night, surrounded by stacks of oversized vodka cans, Amir and I watched videos from the police accountability radicals in Keene, New Hampshire. A sinister sleepover, ours, on Gregory's couch.

"What was Occupy Wall Street like?" Amir asked.

I couldn't tell him. I knew they got Judith Butler to come out and congratulate everyone just for showing up. Then there was the instant museumification of it all. The Smithsonian curators roaming the camps. Rumor was one got a kid under glass like Tilda Swinton.

Look, you whisper, *it's occupying right now*.

In the morning Amir made me wait before we could leave. He smoked some hash from a wooden box at the window and we were on our way. On the city metro an old communist walked onto the rail car in his party buttons and cap. We giggled at him all the way to our stop near the train station.

––––––––––

Eventually, my habits slipped. Like the rest of my company, I slept through the day. At some point during daylight I might wake up and walk across the scattered cat litter to the toilet. Through the window above the water tank I'd see the sheer wall of the opposite flat. I'd cough at the slate universe.

At two in the morning I sent off by email the law school drop form I'd been carrying around with me for weeks. I still planned on taking my exams, but I couldn't stay enrolled in any class that actually kept attendance.

"Just FYI, we're being surveiled," John had emailed.

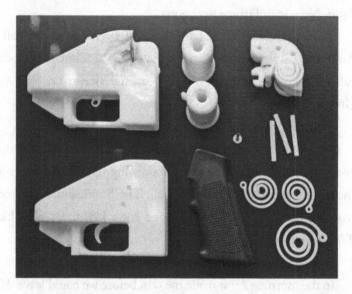

At night Amir and Mihai might bowl into my room, howling like jackals on LSD. I'd slip into the den to do work then, tracking the progress the guys were making back home. On one such night I entered to see Mike Gogulski seated in his bed like the Buddha, naked and cross-legged amid the cigarette butts and empty bottles of tonic water.

"Do you want to live forever?" Mike asked.

"Nah," I said. "I don't think so."

"I don't understand it. You people. You're deathists."

I grabbed Mike's ushanka from a peg and put it on my head. The hat warmed me instantly, and still wearing it, I stepped onto the balcony to return some phone calls. The first was from a guy named Varol. Turned out he was in San Francisco. The call wandered but was fast-paced. He talked about libertarians on oil derricks on the high seas. About old Andrew Carnegie pulling oil out of the ground to a barrel in his basement. I mostly listened to his glib patter and watched the midnight stillness of the street between the flats. I felt like I was being vetted for something.

"We've been watching you now," Varol said, confirming my suspicion. "You want help with this company of yours? You want to do what it takes to really make this happen?"

Despite the salesy tone, I said, "Yeah, I'm interested. Go on."

"You grew up in Texas?"

"Arkansas."

"Sure, Arkansas, even better. You didn't have access to the schooling and resources we did. It's our job to find the three or four guys like you that aren't here but should be here, and kind of air-rescue you. Send the helicopter."

I couldn't think of what to say.

"Tell me you'll come out and visit. We can make DEFCAD what it deserves to be."

Looking through the dark at the naked balconies of the other flat, I just wanted off the call then.

"I'll think about it, man. Thanks for reaching out."

When I returned from the balcony, Mike was still sitting up in his bed, smoking. I walked into the living room while on the phone with an editor of *Defense Review*. Not our first call since I'd been in Europe. Mike turned to listen, so I put the man on speaker just when he began to admit he'd been flirting with anarchism since our initial conversations. When I hung up, Mike was laughing a bit to himself.

"How did you do it?"

"Do what?"

"Figure out how to talk like that."

I looked around. Amir was asleep on the couch, covered in an old American Airlines blanket.

"It's just how I've been doing it, man. What about you?"

Mike blew smoke and squinted past it.

I spoke again, "What makes a man throw off his state like you did? Become a refugee?"

"Well, renouncing my citizenship came first. The Bradley Manning thing was later on," he told me, referring to the campaign he began to aid the troubled private charged with espionage for sending those thousands of Afghan war documents to WikiLeaks.

Mike settled back against his headboard.

"Once upon a time in the late nineties I decided I wanted to leave the US and become a PT—you know, many citizenships. The dotcom money didn't happen. So . . ."

He exhaled another plume of smoke.

"It gets to be two thousand eight. I'm living here a few years. I don't watch much news. It's more like I go through cycles. One year I'm reading no news. Then there's a year where I'm watching things too goddamn much. Watching BBC or CNN and screaming at the television."

I laughed.

"Well, I remember Hillary Clinton saying, 'All options are on the table with respect to shutting down Iran's nuclear program.' And . . . I guess it just hit me then. Why wait for the next bad thing to happen? I started nostate.com as a public record and a method of reinforcement. Now that I've gone out and said I'm going to do it . . ." He let the thought trail off.

The smoke peeked from his lips. And he reached for the glass tray.

"Now, the Manning thing. When the news came out that he'd been arrested, I thought back to the collateral murder video. I got myself very drunk and was very pissed off that this guy had been betrayed. Mainly I was enraged that Lamo had betrayed him to the feds. In a three-day drunken rage I registered the domain. Bradleymanning.org. And . . ." He drew out his final word but didn't go on, leaving that thought hanging there like a fur cap on a peg.

He began to weep.

At last I spoke, feeling as if I understood but suspecting I didn't. I wanted to help him but could think of only one thing that might pass for that. "Get dressed. Come with me."

We walked out and across the icy square of the Tesco complex, stepping over the tram lines and passing slowly under the corner of a stone pavilion. Around another corner we approached a row of old Viennese-style storefronts, now footless under a thickened, white glaze.

"This one's still got food at this hour."

Mike pointed to a confused façade, its pilasters and rusticated corners all painted over in a chalky pink. Beside our entrance was the door to a gaming parlor, whose lit neon and cheap LEDs illuminated the bulky young men in sooty coats who stood smoking beneath them. With dull eyes they measured us as we left them to the cold.

Upstairs we took a table. Mike was in his coat, looking downtrodden.

"These Slovaks," I said. "I mean, it's a hideous race, isn't it? You see it in how they walk, how they carry themselves. Defeat just bred into them."

"I think it's fair to say the legacy of State communism here today is with the people who are past middle age, generally fifty plus, if they're not part of the ruling elite. They've learned a mentality that's beaten down, subservient. No initiative," Mike said.

His eyes searched around while he dragged on the cigarette he'd just lit with the butt of the first. "But they've taught this to their children."

For a while we didn't say much. We listened to the drunken laughter from a table in the corner. There a man fondled a young girl in stripes. Two more wobbled up the stairs in heels and sequined skirts to join them.

"All right. I'll share now."

Mike moved his lip a bit. He didn't look up as I spoke.

"In the forties the War Department commissioned a project with the OSS, the prewar CIA. It's a stamped metal pistol. General Motors made them. I think it was a psychological operation, but the threat isn't credible unless you can use them, right? So they could fire a single .45 round."

I saw his face pick up a bit.

"You pull back a little twist hammer and squeeze. They've got it at a museum in Wisconsin or someplace. There's video of people firing it on YouTube. Brutal little gun. They called it the Liberator."

"What?" Mike grinned.

"They were to airdrop the things along with this little foldout comic strip that shows you how to put it at the base of a soldier's skull. You know, you pop him when no one is looking and take his rifle. But you better get in close."

"And?"

"The US military never really followed through. Maybe they dropped a few thousand. I don't think there's a case of anyone— French Resistance or somebody else—ever using it. But the government never went full-scale. Now tell me why you think that was."

He paused and thought a little, enjoying the game now.

"They were scared to."

"Yeah. That's what I think too."

I was softly nodding then. Happily unaware of the hour, but glad to live there in it.

"Time to drop the Liberator," I said.

In the morning I saluted Mike and hugged Amir.

"You'll meet us in London when you're finished?" Amir asked.

"Of course."

I walked through the alley and over the rails in the street to sit at a bench across from the square. The clock near the supermarket rang noon and gave way to a maudlin little tune on the glockenspiel. In the spitting snow I watched the pretty girls pass with their sad faces. The large, abandoned hotel beyond presided over our affairs peacefully. As I reached for my bags, I whistled "Dixie."

I was on the train to Le Landeron to meet in person the man who'd been primarily funding DD for the past few months. Part of our deal was that I not identify him to the press, but I had taken that secrecy a bit further. I thought of all the things I wanted to say. When I got to Biel/Bienne in the late afternoon, I left the station and walked to a falafel shop. Finding WiFi, I sat for a Huffpost Live interview during which three experts and the underqualified moderator took turns telling me it wasn't possible to 3D-print a gun and how Congress could stop it from happening anyway. I didn't get the chance to talk about the bestiaries that are their site's comments sections—the noises of the abattoir transcribed.

On the train again, now standing, I had a view of a lake in the midlands and could clearly see the Alps. I got a call from back home then. A dean from the law school. Which one? But it's a forbidding list. Squeezed for cash that year, I believe UT law began paying in titles.

She was calling about my add/drop form and didn't like my decision.

I told her it simply came down to attendance. I'd need more flexibility and would not stay enrolled in the class.

"When can you come in to talk about this? Tomorrow?"

"Um." I smiled a little.

"How about Thursday? Wait, are you not here?"

My jaw tightened.

"Where are you?"

I felt the blood pick at my cheeks as I watched the bare streaks of light above a passing chalet.

"I'm abroad . . . but with no disrespect, it's really my business where I am."

"I'm not going to sign off on this, Cody, I'm not. The ABA rules—"

Ah, the professional society. The call was failing. The face reflected before me in the window was a flustered boy's. I turned away, unprepared to see it.

"You do what you have to do," I said. "Look, this is a bad connection. I've sent the documents."

We hissed into a tunnel then. I left the woman and her broken call in the sudden dark.

I was alone at the rural platform, later. As I walked toward a row of closed shops, a tiny car swung in front of me and the driver signaled for me to get in. We went up, up into the Jura and to a mountainous redoubt there. My host gave me a brief tour of the facilities and we sat in an empty room at a card table. I thanked him for largely getting me and DD this far and suggested how much more money I'd need to get the project done.

He hushed me. "The money was always guaranteed. Only tell me what you need as you need it."

We talked of enemies then, and stakes. I told him I thought when I was done it would be the moment of my greatest contempt. A way to throw the Makers, Statesmen, and startup cheerleaders into disarray. He was unimpressed.

In that mountain air we took a walk, talked about immortal palms, and he asked me to peek a bit beyond good and evil. "Think of the world as doomed to this. Or of us as doomed to this world—not the world as we imagine it will be, but the world as it is."

Maybe we were past ideology with this work, I admitted. But I couldn't follow him in that moment. I was unsettled. And not too long thereafter I packed up to leave.

On the train back to Zurich I passed three hours with barely a thought. At some point I remember the car jinked and shifted in a blacked-out trainyard. The harsh cabin lights came on, a signal our journey was ending, I supposed, and the jostling kept us from any ease. All I could see out the window were the floating brand logos. Luminous signs, sailing free from any anchor in all that night. Against the glossy black glass I saw another of my aspects. The slack at his mouth, the dark cast from the brows, a line cut from there out into the cheek. I searched those features a few seconds more, waiting for someone more familiar to appear.

Near the airport hotel I stood slouching in one of the last open shops, turning over a box of painkillers—or what I thought were painkillers—in my hand. When I got to my room, I looked out through the window to the lobby and the strange light show below. I ordered room service and fell asleep beside the tray.

I woke up squinting in the lamplight and staggered into the bathroom to run a shower. While I waited for the water to heat, I sat against a wooden dresser on the floor across from the bathroom doorway, which was wider than I had expected. I studied the roll-in shower, the floor of which was open and undivided across its tiled entirety. I watched the water near the drain in the corner slowly creep to meet the carpet at my feet.

Could I be an operator of the world as it is?

I checked my messages and heard my mother's voice.

It was my birthday.

PART X

Old Street

I reeked, and the others on the plane were not too polite to notice. As I shifted down the aisle, by turns I brushed an arm, a shoulder. I fell into a row of blue seats and covered myself in my bags. In another quarter hour, the half-empty plane was taxied out, and I fell asleep to the German safety presentation. I remember dreaming then.

In my dream I was driving west from the bean field near Little Rock. To my right stood duplicate churches, each absurdly and outrageously proportioned. Then a voice, maybe my own: "And when the clapboards have turned back into cathedrals?"

We landed at Heathrow midmorning, and I wandered only half-awake to the queue at Immigration. I stepped through the crooked river of Bengali luggage at the final exit and hooked a right to the stairwell and the Heathrow underground. On the train, I stared through the grimy walls and overgrown gardens passing outside. Somewhere past Hammersmith my phone began working, and with it my mind.

I went as far as Old Street. In the station was a little bookshop that had a copy of Baudrillard's *Requiem for the Twin Towers*, sitting flat atop its companions in full view. I bought the booklet in cash, sandwiching it between papers in my laptop bag. I spent the afternoon in a Hunan canteen on a side street, listening to the day's news play from a portable television. I rested my packs against the tile wall and handled some business as I ate. Seated a table or two in front of me was an old woman. Her mothball stench rolled into my mouth with every new bite.

That evening I called Amir on a number he must have registered in Spain, and which he picked up only every other time. After circling his block for half an hour, I discovered an abandoned commercial building with an unlit, deeply recessed entrance. In a minute a younger guy worked an iron pole through the tee bars in the glass doors and pried one open just enough to allow me through. I sidestepped to him, and after climbing a junk barrier together, we were in the building's lobby.

Amir stood before us fouled and conducting, like some arcane contractor at the devil's job site. Again he held open his arms for me, now eager to give a tour of the place.

I bid him instead to come outside. "Let's have a meal and talk."

At this, a hidden Mihai roused and scrambled from his slump against a wall to join us returning to the street and its purest cold.

I brought us to a little Italian shop where we ordered bottles of water and full plates of food. As I spoke for the table, the waiter looked down at us with disdain.

Amir sat with his knees up and his laptop over the tabletop. It made a glowing cloud in the dark, which reflected in the glassware and the mirrored bar.

"Tell us of your travels, Master Wilson." Amir giggled.

"I got enough support to finish, I think."

"Ah, congratulations!" His face lit up from the recesses of his hood.

"What have you guys been up to?" I asked.

"We've been at work on a new article for *Bitcoin* magazine. Mihai, we should show him the new cover picture."

We glanced over at Mihai, now grotesquely hunched over his plate, his eating arm working like a piston.

"I want to get some time in with you before I leave, Amir. I want to talk, like you've said, about tools. I know there's something we can do together."

"Yeah, yeah, but let's go back. I want to show you what we are building, free from outside interference—the need to derive profit!"

The diners around us started and turned.

We walked back down a greasy backstreet and paused outside Amir's squat. As before, a small man, this time in oversized pants and a hoodie, jumped the garbage barrier to get the door. Amir told me his name was Santi. Inside, the hanging sheets of vinyl reminded me of when the boys had built a mattress catacombs in my earliest days of dorm life. Amir was talking about the police kettling of European protests. I told him about American "free speech zones." He took me to the higher floors of the squat, each sheltering another tribe with their pillage. I shook hands and exchanged courtesies with the insurgents. Most of them considered themselves the anarchist core of Occupy London, the harder group of activists around whose direct actions the students and casual socialists could rally in fairer weather.

Never able to take root in Paternoster Square, outside St. Paul's Cathedral, or other notable sites, many of them were now here.

On the fifth floor the band there gathered and pointed out their 3D printer to me.

"We're ready to go when you are."

Passing us on the way down the stairs was a dirty blond kid in search of volunteers for a party to head up the street and scout out a new building. These frustrated settlers had received another eviction notice from the London police.

"They tell you two or three days in advance. Then they come and physically remove you."

When we were back to the dusty lobby floor, Santi rolled a hamper forward to Amir, who turned it on its swiveling wheels and lifted up the old laundry to show me the servers and cabling underneath.

"Our mobile infrastructure."

He was a nimble campaigner, our Amir, at home in any situation and proud of his ragged soldiery. He took me inside a harshly lit supply closet, and I slept on one of a pair of couches. When I woke to the cold fluorescence overhead, I saw our company had totally changed save for Amir, who sat exactly as before, still against the bare wall, typing on his laptop. Two girls in dreadlocks joined us as I sat up to watch a bearded man, cross-legged on a mat in the corner, earnestly profess to be the Christ.

Feeling ill, I took another interview call in the basement stairwell. As I waited to speak, I watched the latch windows above and the plunging darkness below. I took in the filth, as the phone filled the spaces with its tinny soundings. At last I grew impatient with the reporter's standard liberal shit.

"Look, you're a good socialist, right?" I thrust out my arm toward the grimy ceiling dropping above me. "Well, we finally got the means of production! What the hell did you think it would look like?"

I couldn't find Amir when I returned, and I wouldn't stay. Without a word I left the squat, searching the orange-tinted streetscapes for a room. I wandered between the sold-out hotels, watching the colors pool in the blacktop further ahead. When at last I found a place, I texted Mihai, who I knew would be giddy to escape and grateful for a real bed.

On TV we watched a Barclays commercial where a hamster in a wheel narrates his life as a common British subject. I sat aghast at the shocking honesty of it all. The banker's billboards in Austin were at least American Schizophrenic. Frost had the courtesy to mix its aggression with professional guilt.

> You Deserve Better.
> We Can't Help You If You Aren't Our Client.

You could watch their building from the rooftop bars on Sixth Street, spot it from under the 35 bridge. A tower of fragmenting crystal, a brilliant carrion flower in icy bloom, threatening to rule us even as we sleep. But they didn't spite you to your face.

Amir emailed the following night to invite us out to radicalize the students at the University College London. Someone had given him a stage to speak. I told a *Slate* reporter I was in town working with Amir and some Occupy activists, and he called back when the Occupy press office asserted that I was, in fact, not. As he heard it, Amir and I were violent psychopaths with no connection to their horizontally organized, inclusive organization. I emailed Adam Wilcox of Occupy London to beg pardon for not signing in with command once I'd made it ashore.

Two days later I checked in at the Sofitel St. James as a scowling, absolute monster. My doubled coats were faded and soiled. My backpack strap had burst and frayed. From behind my sunglasses I watched myself steam in the marble's gleaming black. A pale-faced marauder, multiplied to infinity when the mirrored elevator doors around him closed.

In my room I shed it all. The clothes and bags stayed where they had dropped, and I pulled up to the wooden desk with my laptop. New York State had passed the first sweeping statewide rifle and magazine prohibitions after the shooting in Newtown, naming their work the SAFE Act. I typed quickly. We would call the new printable AR-15 magazine the Cuomo. Divest these politicians of their legacies in the slipstream. In a generation or two, no one would remember the fifty-sixth governor of New York, but someone would be working on or printing out a Cuomo mag. Three times the tolerant liberals got YouTube to remove my announcement video.

The next night I had yet another phone call with the editor at *Defense Review*.

"Cuomo. I can tell you what you did made it to his desk."

"Just congratulating him for making New York safe again."

On YouTube, I saw a video some hillbillies had posted of themselves playing with it. A fan sent me a stunning diary from the *Daily Kos*.

> The only way we can truly be safe and prevent further gun violence is to ban civilian ownership of all guns. That means everything. No pistols, no revolvers, no semiautomatic or au-

tomatic rifles. No bolt action. No breaking actions or falling blocks. Nothing. This is the only thing that we can possibly do to keep our children safe from both mass murder and common street violence.

Unfortunately, right now we can't. The political will is there, but the institutions are not. Honestly, this is a good thing. If we passed a law tomorrow banning all firearms, we would have massive noncompliance. What we need to do is establish the regulatory and informational institutions first. This is how we do it:

This clamor for the truest safety and most glorious compliance. This glittering faith in institutions. To find the author on the street and explain just what was really happening would have been cruel. His world, if it had ever existed, had left him long ago.

———

I stayed in those last days abroad with a girl who went by Claudia, and later Violet. I asked her to take me to the grave of Elizabeth Tudor, but the abbey was closed when we arrived. Near the gift shop I spotted a sculpture of Martin Luther King Jr. among the State church's new additions to its western wall. He stood with the other modern martyrs, in a row looking a lot like a shield, as I thought of it. Safer now in the stone.

I walked Old Street again in the rain, lingered at a bus stop to make a call to Amir, and pulled my coat over my head. Santi cracked open a white door near the street corner. We ascended the stairs and passed through a hole in the wall into a separate terrace. At last we found him on a higher floor. On the whiteboard were bitcoin bounties for breaking high-profile windows about the city.

A larger bounty for tagging the bitcoin symbol on the Bank of London. In his command center, Amir was wearing a fresh mohawk.

"Ah, you're back."

Amir said it like I had only just stepped out.

"I've been writing about costs and living. The way I see it is, like every time we give money to our enemies, we empower them."

"I'm here to say good-bye, Amir."

I studied the papers and garbage tossed about the room, and Amir lording over it all in shoeless comfort. The crazed rebel at ease stepping through the rubble of his dissolute civilization. The gothic journeyman, inspired to go on fashioning weapons from the ruins; willing to use them. He was the deadly fruit of a criminalized generation. I think he wanted the nobility of a death that only some ancient tyrant could have given him. He smiled at me a bit differently, just before I left, as if to say we had worked together after all.

———

At Heathrow I was twice randomly selected for additional screening. At my gate a clipboarded woman in middle age sat with the travelers to make her polite needlings. On the plane, I watched the TV screen. Someone gave *Dumb and Dumber*'s Harry a newsroom and a platform to preach the religion of humanity. Aaron Sorkin writes him on a stage before an assembly, where a college student in the crowd chirps into the mic.

"Tell us why the United States is still the greatest country in the world."

It's not! Harry protests. *But maybe it once was*. Once there had been Great Men. Heroes really, who valiantly brought us the news. Not every piece of information, of course, but what we *needed* to hear. *How* we needed to hear it. Once we had State's Men and we built Great Things.

"But you are"—Harry leans in at her now—"without a doubt a member of the *worst*, period, *generation*, period, *ever*, period."

My nostrils flared. So, Sorkin would marshal the boomer fantasy brigade to judge us in absentia. True to boomer philosophy, a preemptive strike, whereby they revenge themselves on us in advance. As if they knew what was coming.

PART XI

Who Does What to Whom

I had accepted the odd man Varol's invitation to meet in San Francisco. By this time, my position on all the travel was secondary. I was simply going wherever I'd be brought.

"Take an Uber here," he texted when I arrived at SFO. An auspicious start.

After I had looked up just what Uber was, the discourteous bursts of direction continued, and I began to have the tiring feeling, as when I first spoke with Varol on the phone, that I was being simply tested. I arrived at a green, gated apartment complex surrounded by fresh asphalt, off-gassing under an indifferent sun.

Varol buzzed me in and was on the phone when I got to his door. He then quickly motioned for me to sit in his living room, which was littered with packaging, an odd mattress, and an office chair. I opened his fridge while he finished the call at his computer in the bedroom. Energy drinks and bottled water. In another hour he came around the corner to greet me. His dark hair was buzzed short like my own. He looked like at one time he had been in tremendous shape.

"Ah, I thought I had lost you, you know. Did you read the article I sent before you got here?"

"I did."

"Perfect, that will make our time much more productive." He smiled a glitteringly white and orthodonturer smile. "I've lined up a few meetings for us this afternoon. Bring whatever you prepared for your presentation. Are you ready?"

"Yeah, but about the presentation—"

"Let's talk on the way, man."

The surrounding country was tremendous and beautiful. On the highway south I watched the bay trees and the pine. The coastal fog dipped into the hollows. Near Stanford, we made a hasty meeting with a robotics firm and I showed them what DD had been able to do so far without a license. Varol took time to show his own product and his latest graphs, taking me aside afterward and impressing upon me the importance of taking the military entrepreneurial route. When we left, we walked along a campus street and watched the palms.

"Look, I'm about to get you a convertible note for a million bucks, man," Varol told me on this stroll. "You're going to be a millionaire."

At his apartment we made a survey of military contracting businesses, prepping a new business plan for DEFCAD. It was going to be a search engine built as enterprise software and sold to military bases.

"Like it or not, we're talking about Department of Defense here," Varol said, adding "Dee-oh-Dee.

"Otherwise," he went on, "the best you can be is like the Jimmy Wales of the gun movement," referring to the co-founder and promoter of *Wikipedia*.

"Which is something," Varol continued. "But come on! That's not what you're looking for."

At sometime past nine that night we left his place and walked across a wide intersection to a restaurant in a shopping center. The light was dim but the atmosphere lively. With his menu open, Varol shared more of his thoughts.

"When you were in Europe, the way that conversation went, I really didn't think you'd call again."

"Oh, yeah?" I asked.

"There was this article I almost sent you then. You're familiar with the Google founders, Larry and Sergey? Well, according to this article, there was a third founder, or he had a chance to be, anyway. He's a PhD now at some school or other, and one day the press catches up with him and the question was 'How does it feel to not be a billionaire?' He says, 'You know, I finally made peace with it recently.'"

Varol was laughing. "When you said, 'Let me think,' I was like, 'Godspeed, Cody.' Seriously, that's what I was thinking."

———

The next morning, outside a downtown pharmacy, Varol and I met a man known online as Moldbug. Next we drove to a lonely street, where the rows of parking meters lining the rising hill seemed out of place. I followed the pair to a clean and lonely apartment block with an entire terrace wrapped in some kind of metal enclosure. I recall passing through a courtyard and glancing at enormous portholes overhead. Through an inner chamber door, we took off our shoes at the direction of the host who there greeted us. He was a thin man, balding and in his forties. He pointed to a silver end table just as we approached the stair to his loft, issuing the designer's name to no one in particular.

After the stairs we came to a wide room with wooden floors and low seating. Moldbug, representing the Carlyle Club, started the conversation with a thought game he called "Total Domination." Suppose the problem of unrest in Iraq could be solved with suicide collars. Perhaps add drone hive APCs.

For my part, I agreed the old power was diseased. That it no longer had the nerve to do what was required. That it was always secretly complicit with its own defeat. This came off like conservative red meat, I suppose, and the crowd generally assented. When I added that this power would also not be prevailed upon to be replaced, however, the conversation had moved on.

Our host was an investor in a music service, if I remember. As he said it, he was a "VC." This was a town full of them; full of "angels" too. Some others in the room worked for VCs. Our host said he placed his faith in large data sets. Those gathered generally commended the moving front of companies comprising Big Data, who produced the advances necessary for the technologies of the quantifiable self, among other Big Ideas. Varol brought up DD to the gathered company, and our host compared my situation to the one in *Diamond Age*, a novel I hadn't read. Our host doubted a scenario where the United States Government would allow us to release anything that the common people would be able to reproduce.

"Do you really think that if it was possible, they'd let it happen?"

I mustered something about it being too late for the corrupt old republic to get a handle on the problem.

Varol came to my aid. "It's the greatest mistake USG ever made: not licensing the personal computer!"

Moldbug congratulated me. "By the way, bravo on your stupendous media-whoring. I hope you'll get over the anarchism talk soon enough, though. I think you'll find most libertarianism is just born of a frustrated will to power."

I laughed at the point, well made.

"Well," one of them chimed in, "talk of traditional rebellion is fine, but when someone drops that first genetic bomb? Or what if a terrorist is the first to use your printed gun?"

"A system that can stop that is a bigger threat than the threat," I said. Soon we were talking about Sandy Hook Promise.

The next day Varol drove to the Bay through South San Francisco. Before our exit I saw the Zynga building, where the team was no doubt staving off a pandemic of virtual farm foreclosures. Those brave and hoary app makers, forging the economic backbone of our young century.

Near South Beach Harbor was an AT&T carrier hotel with a meet-me room, 641A, built right next to the riser shafts. And somewhere out there, I suppose, was the Dread Pirate. But if you looked hard enough, and could forget about all that, you might just make out the gates to Heaven, designed in Twitter Bootstrap.

I asked Varol, "What do you think about all these soft, sibilant names? Weebly, feebly. Startups or prophylactics?"

Varol laughed. He had been telling me things I had never heard before. The Bay Area libertarians were a small and closeted number. Startup cultures were of different strains. There were men who made millies and there were men who made billies. The rule is to get big and to get big fast, in the name of libertarianism, of course.

"The cities fine your customers tens of thousands of dollars if you're Airbnb; the attorneys general and the unions come after the ridesharing apps. There are undercover cops literally pulling people from Ubers. You have to move to many markets quickly, make it too hard to uproot you everywhere at once."

I met a few more people while I was there. I heard about a man collecting the notes of Peter Thiel to release as a book, about the Massive Online Open Course insurgents trying to drive a wedge between *dot gov* and *dot edu*, about Patri Freidman and those charting the high seas for zones of libertarian secession. What of these seafarers? These sojourners writing our new constitutions in the coffee shops of Palo Alto?

I couldn't explain it then, but they all still seemed to be preaching a Kingdom of Heaven to me. A capitalist salvation. If the Academy taught that the path was through special institutions, Thiel taught that it could be found only by looking within yourself. But these new communards, with their startup barracks and perfect teeth, envisioned for us no workingman's Paris. In San Francisco you might find Capital's radical reformation. The real City of Angels.

"There's room for a character like you out here," Varol told me at one point. "I mean, there's a lot of characters here, but you . . ." I liked these Bay Area libertarians, but most of them deserted me by the time Brendon Eich was thrown out of technology.

I might not have shared Varol's vision, but I was drawn to the novelty of his vocabulary. He was a contrarian, an empiricist, and he promoted a racial realism.

"There's this insistence on mocking the religious for not thinking of humans as evolved animals," he told me, "but then this denial that any of the lessons of evolutionary neurobiology might apply to our observed differences."

He approached political problems pragmatically. Like Lenin, he knew politics simply meant *who does what to whom*.

"As long as you understand the formula, you can achieve the right result."

He compared the USG to Whitman's multitude, and taught me the virtues of assortative mating.

"Take me, for example. I'll be marrying a Chinese woman with an IQ of one seventy."

When I pointed out to Varol that his strategy might lead to social segregation, he didn't disagree. He was about triangulating, understanding the big picture, and finding an exit.

"Journalists and *dot gov* have this odd standoff. Real First Amendment complaints, no access, and there are all these prosecutions of journalists for not giving up their sources. Remember, using the Espionage Act. But the J school set is still quick to align with *dot gov* against the Valley or the wealthy. So, when we do finally start to secede, they will probably fight. They'll mock us, or they'll call us rich. But, my friend, what they don't know is that we'll call them *white*. And they won't be able to overcome it.

"Have you thought of putting girls in your videos?" Varol asked me.

I laughed. "Oh, you mean *girls*."

"Hey, pretty works, and it's cheap."

"How's that?"

"Isn't it obvious? Think about this: move DEFCAD to Estonia, man. You get most of what you can have here, good digital infrastructure. And you pick up a beautiful wife."

Varol taught me other things. Gmail shortcuts. The best Google apps for productivity. That I should always have a whiteboard near to trace out ideas. Wanted levels.

"My biggest concern for you," he said, "is that your wanted levels are too high. You remember *Grand Theft Auto*, right? Wanted levels? You're not going to want to hear this, but a photo of you shaking hands with that congressman always going on about you is the only way you beat back the trouble you have coming."

My favorite of his methods was "switching polarities."

"I'll tell you a story," he said, after we had worked awhile at night. "When I was at Stanford, I took a gender studies class. It was taught by this typical feminist TA, you know. White, shrill, aggressively plain-looking. Day in, day out, overt references to the patriarchy, and I'm the only guy and I never say a *thing*. I'm just looking for smooth sailing, and I need the credit. Well, one day we're assigned a project. The topic is rape. The idea was a direct action against the fraternities to confront the forces of sexism on campus, you know, that fostered this acceptable rape culture. We were even given this police tape too. You know, go cordon off the frat houses. It said something like 'rape-free zone.' And I don't know if you've ever seen these fraternities out here, man."

"Not exactly like those in the deep South, I'm guessing," I said. "Stanford is no Ole Miss."

"No Ole Miss, exactly. The poor guys. Well, anyway, of course these frat guys are helpless in the face of stuff like this. No way to speak out against it. Too timid. Well, this is what I did. I went to the library and the student affairs office and started getting the figures for fraternity rapes on Stanford's campus. You know, through history. I'm thinking maybe one every few years, so I'm digging, and can you guess how many rapes by fraternity men there had been on campus?"

"I don't know, one."

"None. There had never been any! Well, at this point I'm feeling more than vindicated, but I had another idea. So, I come to class the next time we meet and I'm ready. The TA is asking everybody how they did, how good it felt. And I raise my hand. 'Yes.' Very calmly I say to the TA, 'You know, I was in the library and I was looking at the history of rapes by fraternity members on campus. And strangely enough, there weren't any. So . . . I'm all for this direct action, but if we really mean to confront the perpetrators and hold some people to account, I've made a list of blocks in East Palo Alto and Menlo Park where rape and violent crime are out of control. Why don't we go tape off one of those blocks?'

"So, this is East Palo Alto, man. Overwhelmingly Latino and there's poor black neighborhoods, and of course you can guess her reaction. So, her mouth is just wrung into this grimace and she's turning purple. I swear to God, and in a minute she just lets me have it. 'Ah, you're purposefully misunderstanding the point of this action,' and 'How dare you bring up these obviously oppressed communities, and there are systemic and historical factors at issue . . .' And I'm getting just nailed. Everyone is looking at me. But listen. Ha. Ha, listen, I had already expected something like this. I sat there pretty calm. And when she had dressed me down, I looked at her again and said:

"'Well, all I can say is, as a person of color, I'm feeling oppressed right now.'

"She just goes blank, man. Her face turns white. And she just kind of stammers. I had melted her world. Made her into the thing she was programmed to hate. And as soon as she could get it back together, it was this profuse apology. Of course that wasn't her intention, et cetera, et cetera. And for the rest of that semester during each group discussion, I get asked the man-of-color perspective. You flip the polarities."

I laughed, and hard, but I was fading.

"Hey, man, do you need to rest?"

"I just need to lie down."

"Have the rest of the night."

I woke near one a.m. that night, hearing Varol in his room speaking to someone on Skype.

"Yeah, but he's got great verbal intelligence. I think we need to back this guy."

———————

I was invited to a tech meet-up in a misty din downtown. There I met a young, well-dressed economic minister from the Netherlands.

"What do you do?"

"Bitcoin," I answered. "I have a bitcoin project."

Tonight's was a series of timed demonstrations of Google Glass. The first players—contestants?—on the stage showed real-time social networking. You walk into the bar wearing the glasses and scan the crowd, finding thumbnail profiles of interest, potential romantic matches. They broke down the tech quickly.

After a couple more presentations came an awkward wunderkind. He spoke and moved in a way that said he assumed we'd all seen him before, that we were all familiars who'd indulge or, at the very least, forgive him. As soon as he properly began, he was running out of time. But for the lovable wunderkind, everything is forgiven. With seconds to spare, he turns on a lightbulb with his voice. The crowd cheers.

These people didn't believe anything, I thought. I remember hearing about the "Singularity" around this time. An idea, promoted by an engineer at Google, that soon the rate of human technical progress would reach such a point of dizzying speed and expansion that humanity itself would be lost in the explosion. Even annihilated. This little show was just a burlesque of the end of metaphysics.

Join we, the transhumanists, and celebrate the joys of dis-incarnation. Polite society won't let us believe in anything but our own pointlessness, but have a look, one day the entire "human" concept will be forgotten.

As if people hadn't stopped being the reason for things long ago.

"Mark," someone from the audience asks of the wunderkind, "how would you describe what you do?"

Proudly now. With conviction: "I make the future."

A burst of applause. I moved off the column near the bar and walked for the bathroom, unable to take the praise for this dandy who, to the uninitiated gun printer, was something less than the sum of his awkward physical bits. At the urinal, I noticed the bathroom was as characterless as those assembled without. I took a pen from my bag and wrote on the wall, completing the most transgressive act to have ever occurred in the building.

The minister got my attention as I moved to make my way out of the assembly.

"You're leaving?"

"Afraid so."

I paused after I turned to the stair, and stepped back to whisper to him. "The currency wars are here. The great States are pitted against each other. We'll work with any government that wants an advantage."

He quickly handed me his card.

PART XII

Wine-Dark

At the end of February, DD had a fair amount of bitcoin. I set the video of our lower receiver's fourth revision to Ravel's "Bolero," and posted it to the development blog with the caption "DD welcomes Congress back from vacation."

A fan sent a video of Rachael Maddow throwing a fit at this. "Look at it not failing," she said with that trademark mock incredulity.

What irked her, I believed, even more than our happy contempt, was the ease with which we had our story told: that it was being told the way we wanted it told.

By the same token, this pleased the gunnies without end. I got a phone call from an unknown number:

"Cody Wilson? Hoo! I love the stuff you boys are doing."

"Ha, is that right?"

"Yep, I'll tell you what. We've got a bump fire stock we're working on out here in Houston. Say we send you one to put on video. For free. Don't you know that'd get 'em going?"

"It's an interesting offer," I said, sitting back in my upstairs office chair. "Here's my counter, if you don't mind. I'll put the stock on video if you let me copy the design and put it up on DEFCAD for the people to download."

I could hear his smile disappear.

"It had been weeks since a call like that," I told Ben later that night on the phone.

"Who are the real communists anymore?" Ben responded. "We should be charging tuition! The spooks listening to these calls should be getting college credit! Do you remember that Napster poster from back in the day?" he continued. "Like it was presented by the Recording Industry Association of America itself. It's a demon Lenin with his hand on the shoulder of some kid at the computer. It says, 'Remember, when you pirate MP3s, you're downloading communism!'"

Varol flew into Austin the next week for South by Southwest, a local tech conference held in March. He found an apartment on Eleventh Street with Airbnb, a service he mentioned to me more than a few times.

"Austin is already moving against this," he told me when I caught up with him. "Fines for homeowners running unlicensed hotels. It's on." He was in a fine mood.

We stayed in his rented apartment the night before my scheduled speech at the conference to finish the new concept behind DEFCAD, but I was determined to at last duck this enterprise idea; to turn it into something nonmilitary. A search engine, fine, but for the public. We worked together through the night. He on the crowdfunding site, and I on the video.

What does 3D printing mean? And can it be subversive?

The little clip had become personal to me, more my ode to the technology than a sales pitch. More optimistic and sentimental in tone than anything I had yet allowed myself to make. I look back on it in real wonder now, knowing I personally felt none of its optimism while making it. Varol fell asleep around three in the morning, and sometime before six I released the presentation online.

In the Sunday *Times* Evgeny Morozov called the whole concept creepy. From his civil society point of view, he was afraid all this "openness" and "access" was ultimately depoliticizing. That it didn't mean anything because it could mean anything. He felt democratic sovereignty was at stake in letting people look up their own 3D gun files on the Internet. And he was right in a way. But then, the great democracies were just as preoccupied with the destruction of popular authority as I was. Had he missed it, our collective lapse into middling technocracy? The *political* he strained to eulogize was already well lost. Every inherited institution was in shadowfold.

Thrusting a gun onto the Internet seemed to be an act of singular decision to me. Absolute and irrevocable. More vibrantly political than any recent event I could recall. Tell every quasi-governmental committee, write every white paper you want, but the guns would be there. Shot into orbit.

A reporter named Uwe followed me around after the conference. I kicked up my feet on a boxed metal detector I had shipped to my apartment from Korea, and we talked about soft tyranny and voluntary servitude. When I got distracted, he grasped his forehead and pressed at his temples. I took him to a shooting range, Best of the West in Liberty Hill, to watch one of our rifle receivers at work. I would turn around after a few rounds to see him sunning himself with his eyes closed.

When I told him that I got my firearms manufacturing license in the mail, he didn't quite believe it. "But why would they give it to you? They know what you intend to do."

Shaking the blue-and-white license in my hand, I proclaimed, "I told them I was starting a business! They want to ban every gun, sure, and in a month they'll do it. But that doesn't touch commercial manufacturing. This country wails for an end to the pain. The machine must be brutal and destroy any who disagree. But if you tell it you are an agent of the accumulation of capital, then *everything* is permitted."

Later that day, I drove out to a quiet spot nestled between the houses in Hyde Park. Under a shade tree I parked and called my father. While I spoke, I stared at an orange bumper sticker on the back of the SUV ahead of me. A uterus and ovaries. "Come and Take It."

"Tomorrow I'm going down south to set up the metal detector at our new gun shop with John."

"Well, do you boys even know how to work a metal detector?"

"I mean, it came with a manual," I said. "How hard could it be?"

My father laughed with a gentle bewilderment. The wordless confirmation of what we'd all known: that this little project had gotten far too bizarre and far too involved.

"As far as I see it, it's just the best cover," I said. "When the hammer does come down, we can say we literally took every legal step to print and test the thing. I mean, they're watching."

I was mostly referring to the undercover cop who was now

parked across the street from my apartment every day. But I had kept my father up on all the government visitors to our websites. The rumor that DHS was monitoring us out of Dallas.

"It's weird thinking you're being watched," I told him. "After a while you have to make a stupid peace with it. You even hope that at some point your selector likes you, or if he can't like you, is at the very least capable of the occasional sympathy."

I don't think he knew what to say.

"I know we're supposed to outgrow the idea of guardian angels, but maybe—like in old myths, how everyone has a doppelganger or could be responsible for someone else's life—you can even hope that your monitor might steer you away from trouble. Maybe in rare moments he wants what's best for you."

I never meant to hurt nobody. Google as my witness.

That night my sleep was wine-dark and dreamless.

———

A day trader named Robert had heard my call online for more objects to put into blueprints. He invited me to his house downtown, off East Street, and I found him behind a construction site across from an elementary school. He met me at his screen door and asked me in while he fetched the rest of his arsenal. Over the glass top of his wooden desk he laid out modified AKMs and Saiga magazines. He had extended Glock mags and spare stocks and I told him it all felt serendipitous. We'd just begun work on printed AK magazines.

"I had one last month drawn up by a kid from *4chan*," I told him. "Garbage, but I guess that's what I should have expected. I started over with a guy in Louisiana, and the first new one is getting printed tomorrow. Do you want to bring your rifle and help me test it this weekend?"

I walked back to my car with Robert's rifle pieces and mags in a cardboard box. That evening I had them on FedEx trucks to volunteers from across the country. DD's glory boys. Before nightfall, I bought a cheap Bulgarian AK mag from a local shop near Manchaca and gave it to a kid who agreed to meet me on campus. We did the exchange right at the foot of the Tower.

Robert texted in the morning for the plan, and I told him we'd have some special guests. The Russian network NTV would be in town to meet us at Best of the West. Robert was all too happy to make an appearance.

First the crew and I went to Brian Bauman's place, just like a dozen times before. I asked to sit while they filmed. We watched the AK magazine rise from the photopolymer goo, and in another hour or so we were at the range. But when we got there, the new magazine didn't fit Robert's rifle. Feeling faint, I left Robert and the rifle line and sat on a boulder outside the range office, carving at the magazine with my keys again, cursing myself for growing careless. I looked up and couldn't see my car, eclipsed by so many glinting trucks in the white gravel parking lot.

When the NTV correspondent came out to check on me, I begged her pardon and walked inside the range's office. My sight went gray and I dropped to my knees over the bathroom toilet, losing everything. When I stepped out again, the blood pounding back into my hands, I kept talking about another appointment. The correspondent and her cameraman tried by turns to comfort me or understand what was happening, but I waved them off.

"I'm sorry. That's our time. I'm sorry."

I fell into my car seat and onto the makeshift saddle skirt I'd made from a falsa blanket. I sifted through the spare change in my cupholder, the spent casings and lottery tickets—for what?—and I sent down my windows to let the pocket of heat flee the cab. I watched my gearshift for a moment, flaking like an old salt pan, then I bit back the taste of acid and gunpowder and headed south.

_____

My old friend Daniel Bizzell from Arkansas surprised me with a visit that next week. It had been months since I'd seen him in person. We'd spoken only by phone when it was time for the DD board to meet and approve a legally problematic course, which was happening more and more often now. I showed him the broken rifle pieces. The half-built MakerGear kit at the bar. The spools of nylon filament that I kept above the dryer. After he had gotten up that morning, his socks were dirty.

"Hey, when was the last time you cleaned this place?" he asked.

On his first full day in Austin I asked Daniel if he wanted to meet Alex Jones. It took near an hour to get down there in the traffic, but in a quiet commercial complex we found a low, stretched-out compound with darkened windows, indistinguishable from those surrounding. We parked at a corner and took the simple sidewalk to a locked and blacked-out door. _Infowars_ reporter Jakari Jackson let us in.

"Break down the history here," Alex started, when we were seated in the studio during his radio show. "The history of how this started and why it's sent shockwaves through the system, Cody."

"You mean the printable gun idea?"

He boomed in the microphone, his eyes somehow separate and with a sublime equanimity. "The printable gun idea, and the ATF getting involved and everything that's happened."

"Yeah. This is going to be and is right now a symbol of the reversibility of institutional control of property, specifically dangerous property like the firearm. And we know that there's been a multigenerational effort, especially in the twentieth century, to take the battle rifle out of the hands of Americans. The battle rifle as the birthright of patriotic Americans, out of their hands. This is a sign of the reversibility of that entire program."

Jones looked on approvingly, then spoke. "And we'll show people a document cam shot of that rifle right there who are watching on TV."

The rifle wobbled a bit in his hands. I eyed it on a monitor over our heads.

"The lower receiver you see there in white," I said. "This is not an SLA-printed piece, and the distinction is important. This is actually a very cheaply made fused-deposition-modeling printed piece. This is a kind of piece you could make yourself with an Ultimaker or a MakerBot, machines that are less than five thousand dollars, sometimes less than two thousand. And the piece itself costs less than twenty dollars . . . and that's an expensive way to make that piece."

Jones tangled with the magazine. On his desk sat an enormous anti-materiel rifle.

That night Daniel showed me an article from the UK *Telegraph*.

Why do I not believe Mr. Wilson is dangerous? Well, while I greatly admire his ability to publicise his company world-wide, I just don't think the technology is anywhere near ready to make his dreams a reality. To quote one manufacturing engineer, "Home 3D printers are cheap toys for making more cheap toys." Firearms are dangerous, and require incredible tolerances and perfect adjustment to work.

I sat back in my chair. "This is the single best piece to show how far the British have abstracted guns outside of their own experience. You saw it a couple of months ago, I'm sure, an AK made from a shovel! And if you believe the stories, the original was made in a train yard the same way."

Bizzell was laughing. "Read some more of it."

I think it's so unlikely that, if Mr. Wilson can home 3D print a whole assault weapon by the end of the year, I will happily fly to Texas and he can shoot me with it. I've still got my BBC-issue flak jacket so, worst-case scenario, I'll find out if your licence payer's money has gone to good use.

"What are you going to tell him?" Daniel asked.

I started smiling. "I'll tell him to google what a flak jacket is."

On the second day of Bizzell's visit, we were visited by a friendly reporter from PJ Media, a conservative commentary website. I showed him our magazines and a rifle, which now had a .22 casing through the printed lower for a front takedown pin.

"And you're sure we can't go shooting today?" he asked us. "I'd be happy to come along."

"It's just not in me today, brother."

That night we talked about Christopher Dorner, the shootings, and his suicide in that cabin in the mountains of San Bernardino. He believed that the Los Angeles Police Department had unjustly fired him because he'd been willing to cross the thin blue line and report on his fellow officers' use of excessive force.

"I didn't want that body they found to be him," Bizzell told me.

"I kept thinking it would be like in the Bourne movies. After the fire he calls up the LAPD chief on the phone."

"Hey, Charlie."

"Chris? Where are you, Chris? You need to come in."

"Get some sleep, Charlie. You look tired."

That afternoon we took a trip down to Regal Row near Manchaca, and I showed Daniel the gun-printing closet I was renting with the help of our engineer, John. A closet was all to which it could truly amount.

"Hey, it looks like this stone wall is about to fall over," Bizzell said, pointing to the façade over the entrance to the place. I was fussing with the key in the door. As it had no handle, I pulled it open by the rusting iron grate that covered its former window. This was itself stuffed with sun-bleached magazines.

"Potential lawsuit," I said. "Leave it."

I showed Daniel the concrete floor of the place, just large enough for him to enter as well and neither of us to sit comfortably. I pointed to the gun safe, which I had already managed to break.

"John and his brother painted the place while I was in Europe. They punched a hole there," I said, pointing to the wall, "for a fan and to run the power to the new printer we got."

"Where is the printer?" Daniel asked.

"I thought it would be here today. John takes it back and forth to his place. He's printing trigger assemblies."

"So, this is where you think it's going to get done?"

"Yeah, from what I've seen, John is going to get us there. The FDM materials are ironically cheaper and better for doing it. Like I said, the outstanding question is barrels, and we'll head out to test those soon enough."

We stood in the parking lot for a while before we left, glancing at a passing train and listening to the cicadas.

On the third day I came downstairs in the early afternoon to find Bizzell still asleep on the couch. "Hey, wake up. We've got a call with the IRS in a second."

Bizzell sat up and leaned over his knees for a bit.

When the agent called, I put him on speaker. "All right, so, I've been assigned your nonprofit application and I am now notifying you that I will be sending a detailed list of questions."

"Okay, sounds good," I told the agent.

"I'll share them with you now, and please look them over carefully when they arrive by mail. From that time you'll have thirty days to respond."

"All right, what would you like to know?"

For a half hour we ran through the questions and enjoyed the easygoing nature of the call.

"Well, okay, then," the agent said at last. "I think that puts us on a good footing, so . . . look for a call from me again in about . . . one year."

Bizzell and I looked at each other in awe.

On the fourth day of Daniel's visit we drove to Waco. After some minutes outside town, the farm road shriveled and worsened.

"And where are we going?" Daniel asked.

"I've been meaning to do this for a while. Keep a lookout to the right."

We came to a stone gate and pulled through the open iron doors. On a potholed, gravel road I eased the car along. Daniel could see a stone monolith.

"This is Mount Carmel."

Ahead of us stood an overweight family waiting still outside their dusty van. They studied a stack of square stones mortared into a simple, angled wall dotted here and there with flowers. We pulled past this monument and the drive circled to a tiny white chapel before a large field of tall, bright-green grass. The sun was out.

We left the car and walked to where the grass was thinner toward the old footprint of the buildings. A black groundskeeper in a light jacket was at work with his weed eater farther afield.

Daniel and I walked the support wall of a basement shelter, its ceiling long collapsed, which was filled with stagnant water. Studying the backfield, we saw an old telephone pole that must have presided over the siege.

It had heard them play Nancy Sinatra by night.

"These boots are made for walking . . ."

Heard the assault vehicles blaring that this was, in fact, not an assault.

I walked back to the chapel to take one of the printed maps, a reminder of the compound that stood and burned here. As Bizzell approached, I listened to the wasps at the eaves and the little gas engine in the field. The family was still at the tiny monument nearer the gate. I walked off the chapel's porch and to a headstone at the road in red granite, which read:

> *I saw under the altar the souls of them*
> *That were slain for the word of God and*
> *For the testimony which they held*
> *And they cried with a loud voice saying*
> *How long O Lord Holy and True dost thou*
> *Not judge and avenge our blood on them*
> *That dwell on the earth?*

PART XIII

Undetectable

On April Fool's Day I left Indianapolis. I had stopped by not long after Bizzell left Texas to see one of my oldest friends, perhaps for the last time. We talked about Amir, the fascists in San Francisco, and the tiny gun-printing shop out at Regal Row. I said we'd print the gun by the end of the month, and that I didn't think I'd be back.

I kept my phone off after waking that morning and on the way to the airport. Passing to my gate, I walked through a short hall filled with the stinging sounds of an alarm. The TSA agent slumped over her podium told me to be calm.

"It's not you, don't be worried."

"I'm not."

The night before, I had asked Haroon to post a little picture on our websites.

This domain name associated with the website DefenseDistributed.com or Defcad.org has been seized pursuant to an order issued by a U.S. District Court.

A federal grand jury has indicted several individuals and entitites allegedly involved in the operation of DefenseDistributed.com and related websites charging them with the following federal crimes:

Conspiracy to Violate the Arms Export Control Act (22 U.S.C. § 2778), Conspiracy to Violate the Undetectable Firearms Act (18 U.S.C. § 922(p)), Conspiracy to Commit Money Laundering (18 U.S.C. § 1956(h)), and Criminal Copyright Infringement (18 U.S.C. §§ 2, 2319; 17 U.S.C. § 506).

Yes, the jackboots had finally got DEFCAD. At a Midas in West Little Rock, a woman in a Kony 2012 shirt watched Wolf Blitzer report this as news.

Between flights back to Austin, I powered on the phone to find voicemails from NBC, CNN, and Mr. Alex Jones, who said, "Cody. I need to know what happened here. We're going to go live with this if I can't get you to call me back by the afternoon."

At last in the Bergstrom parking lot, I walked for my car just listening to the rest of my messages. Some were from good and honest people, whom I didn't mean to distress. But maybe they'd excuse a little prescience.

I turned my phone back on the next day to see the UN had passed a multilateral treaty to prevent and eradicate all illicit trade in conventional arms. Well, damn. So, the civil society had saved the world after all. One less thing, I guess. I spent the rest of the day watching the new download logs at DEFCAD.

A week before my next trip, someone sent me a letter DCCC chairman Israel had been circulating.

```
Co-Sponsor Legislation to Ban 3D Printed Guns
From: The Honorable Steve Israel
Date: 4/10/2013

Co-sponsor the Undetectable Firearms
   Modernization Act

Dear Colleague:
  I urge you to co-sponsor legislation I
introduced today to give law enforcement the
tools they need to protect American families
from firearms and gun components that come
straight off a 3D printer. My legislation
would extend and update the ban on guns and
gun parts that cannot be detected by metal
detectors or x-ray machines, entitled the
Undetectable Firearms Modernization Act.
The original Undetectable Firearms Act
was passed in 1988 when a plastic gun was
science fiction, and now that technology has
advanced to a point where these guns are being
developed to fire bullets, Congress must act
to extend this ban. Below I have included a
recent CNN piece that describes the issue and
intent of my legislation.
  Defense Distributed, a group based in Austin,
Texas, has been working since late last year
towards a single goal: using a 3-dimensional
printer to manufacture a plastic firearm.
So far the group has been successful in
```

manufacturing a fully plastic, fully functional lower receiver for an AR-15, the same gun used in the Sandy Hook shooting, as well as high capacity magazines for the AR-15 and AK-47. Recently, the group's founder has stated that they will be able to produce a working 3D printed gun by the end of April. These developments beg the question—what good will gun safety laws do if guns and gun parts can be printed in a basement using plans found online?

The Undetectable Firearms Modernization Act would update current law and extend key provisions to include both lower receivers and magazines printed in plastic by individuals. The legislation specifically targets individuals who produce plastic gun components and magazines, while exempting legitimate manufacturers. Extending this ban is necessary to give law enforcement the tools they need to keep plastic guns that can slip through security lines off of our streets.

Sincerely,
STEVE ISRAEL
Member of Congress

The Kansas State chapter of the Young Americans for Liberty flew me out to speak that month. Their club vice president, a kid with messy hair and glasses, found me near baggage claim. I walked with him and his friend to their car, and we loaded up to head for town. Down the highway, I watched the sun fall below the trees. The kid spoke up.

"Sorry about all the confusion and the last-minute confirmation."

"Yeah, what happened there?" I asked.

"Well, we had actually dropped you from the schedule a couple months ago."

I smiled out the window. "And why was that?"

He laughed nervously. "You're a divisive guy, some would say. The board and some of the speakers said it was a mistake to have invited you."

The kid looked in the rearview back to his friend.

"But then we changed the board."

After nightfall they dropped me at a hotel, saying all was taken care of. At the desk, the receptionist asked for my reservation.

"Under Wilson, probably."

She worked for a bit at her keyboard.

"I'm not seeing anything under that name, sir."

"Maybe Young Americans for Liberty. They've got a thing here tomorrow."

"Hmm. I'm sorry, sir. There's nothing here."

I handed her my credit card.

I came down in the morning with my laptop and the same clothes from the night before. I grabbed a cup of coffee outside the conference rooms and, putting on a name-tag sticker, noticed I was the only person not in a suit. But the groups of students did mix handily. Young preprofessionals and polite student politicians, in dress and demeanor every bit another constituency of the Republican Party.

Tom Woods, the libertarian historian and author, was speaking that day, along with a guy from the Flint Hills Tea Party. I had arrived at my scheduled time to the conference room, happy to look over so many Union volunteers. I showed them slides of our epoxy AK magazines and stills of a printed .380 barrel just tested out in the dirt at Lockhart. Not only had it worked once, but ten, even eleven times.

I told them it wasn't yet a crime to think politics without State. They didn't have to mortgage their idealism and youth so soon. They didn't have to be so eager to huff the tainted breeze off the Potomac.

When the talk was over, I sat for a local paper and talked to a few guys, one of whom brought me more coffee.

"You're Miseseans? I assume by the bow tie," I said, pointing to the neckwear most associated with the followers of the Ludwig von Mises Institute, an enterprise dedicated to promoting the Austrian school of economics.

The boy laughed, covering the offending tie unconsciously with his hand.

"I have a friend who's always on about Mises," I continued. "He says it's radical, even revolutionary, in this society to just save up capital. You acquire and build the base of a solid business and way of life, and you sap the State. Working hard makes you a friend of freedom. Tell me he's just joking."

The young men were apologetic. It wasn't fair of me to rag on them, though.

Before I left by taxi, a student caught up to me in the hotel parking lot.

"I just wanted to speak on behalf of my friends. This was such a breath of fresh air. We were all asking, where have you *been*?"

"I guess I was just minding my own business." After smiling, I thought better of what I'd said. "Maybe I was listening."

I made it to the tiny municipal airport, where CNN was on the TVs at the corners of the miniature concourse. A manhunt was under way for bombers who had hit the Boston Marathon. The people could be seen shrieking "Boston Strong!" And the residents in a little neighborhood held open their doors for the shock troops, rooting them on from behind as they stormed around their kitchens. No doubt enjoying the service, some even tweeted their receipts.

I walked to the desk to buy a ticket home.

"I'll need to run a check first, sir, before I can sell you a ticket."

Below my glasses the smile left my face. "And why is that?"

"Well, you're a young male, traveling alone, buying a one-way, same-day ticket. Frankly, sir, you match a profile."

I had out my ID.

"Do it, then."

I waited alone in the sunlit concourse, tired of watching Jake Tapper and the blinking vending machines and the spotless tile floor. When my phone buzzed, I saw the Manchin-Toomey amendments to a background-check bill had died in the Senate. The effort was six votes short. There wasn't going to be new federal gun control.

Still waiting to purchase my ticket, I called Ben to listen to him boil. "A victory. But so what? In New York they insisted the schemes were never going to be about databases. And yet here we are. Of course it was always about the lists and criminalizing the law-abiding. Even now the states are considering approval schemes for the transfers of the object's physical custody between two people in the same room. A form, a check, and a waiting period every time you'd like to hand the piece to another human being."

"Mmm," I concurred. "Intercept the culture and invert the people's attitude toward their own instincts. They want to send us to that half gloom on Sipsey Street. Drive us to a crazed despair. And legality is their favorite little baton."

Ben was still going on. "Glorious compliance! Controlling the whole of the social to get to the guns. It's like 'nicotine is the drug, but we regulate tobacco.'"

"Isn't that the evil genius of e-cigs, then?" I asked.

"It's smoking that's banned in public, not the cigarette. The e-cig isn't banned for health reasons but because it makes compliance and transgression equivalent. Even to *simulate* rebellion is a threat. A purer terror even, free of substance."

Ben was chuckling as I posed a question. "Say we don't quite get there? The gun doesn't work. Wiki Weapon is a failure, they're all right about it. We release a mock pistol anyway. You simulate the catastrophe. Don't you still trip the entire machinery into motion?"

"Ha-ha, how could you not?"

I was looking back at the TV.

"This bomber kid has Twitter fangirls. Did you see that?"

————

I returned to Austin and drove into town, more frustrated with the idea of being watched than before. Surveying the busy parking lot from a stone shelf outside a Best Buy, I called the Institute for Justice to plead with Clark Neily on the phone. A member of the Texas Bar, he was also the director of IJ's Center for Judicial Engagement. He'd written a book on the same subject.

"But isn't there something I can do to slow it down? Frustrate them a little."

"Not a whole hell of a lot, Cody."

I took the elevator to the fifth floor of the law library and walked through the cool and glassy maze of faculty offices. The central stairway and the walls surrounding were awash in skylight. I sat sweating against the wall across from Professor Mitch Berman's door. He was my criminal law professor during my first year at UT, and he was gracious enough to let me bounce a problem off him. Within the hour I sat in front of his desk.

"Well, it seems you're quite the celebrity these days."

"I was hoping you could help me with something." And together we read the Undetectable Firearms Act:

(p)(1) It shall be unlawful for any person to manufacture, import, sell, ship, deliver, possess, transfer, or receive any firearm
   (A) that, after removal of grips, stocks, and magazines, is not as detectable as the Security Exemplar, by walk-through metal detectors calibrated and operated to detect the Security Exemplar; or
   (B) any major component of which, when subjected to inspection by the types of x-ray machines commonly used at airports, does not generate an image that accurately depicts the shape of the component. Barium sulfate or other compounds may be used in the fabrication of the component.

(2) For purposes of this subsection—
   (A) the term 'firearm' does not include the frame or receiver of any such weapon;
   (B) the term 'major component' means, with respect to a firearm, the barrel, the slide or cylinder, or the frame or receiver of the firearm; and

> (C) the term 'Security Exemplar' means an object, to be
> fabricated at the direction of the Secretary, that is—
>> (i) constructed of, during the 12-month period be-
>> ginning on the date of the enactment of this subsec-
>> tion, 3.7 ounces of material type 17–4 PH stainless
>> steel in a shape resembling a handgun; and
>> (ii) suitable for testing and calibrating metal detec-
>> tors:

We went over it twice, diagramming the sections. "But my real question is this," I said. "If you'll look at section three—"

> . . . this subsection shall not apply to the manufacture, posses-
> sion, transfer, receipt, shipment, or delivery of a firearm by a
> licensed manufacturer or any person acting pursuant to a con-
> tract with a licensed manufacturer, for the purpose of examin-
> ing and testing such firearm to determine whether paragraph
> applies to such firearms. The Secretary shall ensure that rules
> and regulations adopted pursuant to this paragraph do not
> impair the manufacture of prototype firearms or the develop-
> ment of new technology.

When the professor looked up, I began. "It seems that Congress has allowed a safe harbor for manufacturers to test guns that might violate the law to see if they do in fact meet the standards in the law. I read that these rules would have protected prototyping as well. But the secretary *never made* the rules, and then neither did Justice when the ATF was folded into them. So, my question is, in the absence of those rules, is this whole provision void?"

"Well, that's the right question," Professor Berman replied, after a moment's pause. "If the law says 'Justice shall determine,' and then Justice does not determine, does that mean DOJ has nullified the safe harbor provision? I think you can make a very good case that it does mean that."

I had first discovered this problem with the mechanics of the law while on the phone with a Westlaw representative. We looked for anything in the *Code of Federal Regulations* to modify the UFA, but there was nothing. This "law" had existed for twenty years and more, and now I found out there was nothing behind it. No way to seriously navigate it. An honest-to-God Potemkin law.

The Westlaw rep was bemused, telling me that she saw the same kind of problem within environmental legislation and regulation a lot, but was surprised to find it here in Title Eighteen code. But I got over the shock soon enough. This government understood simulation better than any of us. Power must arrive and make pronouncements most especially where no power actually exists.

Seeing that I was no less dissuaded from acting, having learned I had no great legal advantage, Professor Bergman spoke deliberately. "Be very careful, now. We're talking about a real crime with real consequences. You may not want to do what you have in mind."

"Yeah, well, it's happening," I said. I couldn't help but laugh a little. Giddy with the stinging sense of my own doom. "And no one is ready for it."

"Yes, that may very well be." The professor kept his hands clasped under his chin as I stood from his desk. "But are you ready for it?"

———

The next week I was in Brian Bauman's garage out at Mustang Mesa for an interview with CNBC's Brian Sullivan. In the setup the anchor talked more about getting to the F1 track and playing with his race car than about our operation. My own Brian and the producer watched from a monitor outside the room. With the lights on, he got to work.

"But Cody, we've just toured the ATF offices and they're still using a paper filing system. You guys are light-years ahead with this tech. Don't you think you're overreacting with this antigovernment thing?"

This was exactly two months before Snowden. "Snowed In," Ben would text me.

I held Sullivan's gaze a bit longer at that question, as if in the extra second I'd get an apologetic shrug and a wave to continue. Neither came.

"Yeah, a plastic automatic might seem pretty wicked. But the autopen is mightier."

It was just us, the camera, the machine, and its goopy, evil matter. I avoided the landmines, found a couple of flourishes, and soon everyone was shaking hands and packing. Brian and I stood in the garage to wave as we watched them back out of his driveway. He spoke out of the side of his mouth without looking at me.

"That producer was cursing at the monitor in the other room. When you were in there with Speed Racer. Incredible."

"What, are you saying she was coaching him through the questions?"

"I'm telling you, man! In case you needed any more proof. There's no more real journalism."

When we walked back into his shop, Brian took down a box of magazines from a wooden shelf. He placed it on the worktable, pulling one out and under the light for our examination.

"I think they're not working so well because the material has a low temperature resistance. 'Cause you know here they're doing well." He waved to indicate the space around us in the fan-cooled garage.

"But in the heat or the sun they're changing dimensionally, and it's interfering with the spring release. But check this out."

Now Brian held up another magazine, black and grainy with a lone star on its side.

"That's nylon," he said. "I think the ultimate tech for you will be laser sintering with nylon or nylon composite."

I drove back late that night with the new magazine added to the strange lot of relics in my trunk, but if I should have been excited, I wasn't. John's secret work on the Liberator was nearly finished now. We'd been testing concept pieces for over a month. I didn't want to tell Brian that I figured we were almost at the end of our road. When we released the printed pistol, I felt the feds would finally step in and we'd never be able to do this kind of work again. As I watched the storming sky off to the south, I knew I'd never even use Brian's magazine.

But I didn't need to use it, really. If done right, the printed pistol would prefigure everything else like it to ever come. In one revelation a permanent phantasmagoria. A terrible omen of a new and unwinnable West.

The tollway carried me south in silence. Without another thought I watched the heat lightning, high and away, in its masterful, bleary violence. Further out were the orange halos of the high masts, which now looked cast over the trembling city, as if sent to protect it from the soundless calamity overhead, and unaware I was among them.

Under the spoiling orange moon, John and I drove north on Highway 1 and to 183. We passed the Echelon building, where Joseph Stack had sent the IRS his pound of flesh. John was trying to update me quickly. The concept was finished, but the printer was broken.

"Our guy couldn't fix it on his own. We're going to have to get Stratasys to come service it."

"Can you hide it like we talked about?"

We agreed. The printer would hide out in the body shop beside the gun-printing closet to fool the corporate repairman.

"Are you not worried now?" John asked. "I mean, this is the part where they send us the national security letter. Or where you get disappeared."

"This ex–Special Forces guy started emailing me a couple months ago," I said. "We talk now, and the other day he tells me about NATO bombing Yugoslavia and how much it slowed down MySQL commits. Serb developers would just never be heard from again on the email list."

Then, more directly to his question, I said, "I still don't feel like I've risked a thing. There's been no opportunity to put our lives into play. Don't you want a chance to show them you're serious?"

John was watching the sleepy street. "I want to thank you," he said after a long few moments of silence.

"What? Why?"

"When we first started working together, I thought, well, this is all a mechanical engineering problem. And I'm an electrical engineer. They don't need me. It was cool to meet and talk and all that, but I didn't think I'd be able to help. I was interested in solving the problem, but I didn't feel qualified."

John paused. "But that day we were out with the magazines, I got it. We were dumping graphite into my M16—ah, that was killing me—but it was clear. Those kinds of costs didn't matter. This was exactly what I wanted. I thought no, I'm not an ME, but here I am fixing this problem. And I'm just glad that I had that M16, because it was the excuse for all of this to now happen."

In Lockhart John and I tested printed barrels with a modified Remington 870. We faced a black-and-white block fastened to an aluminum cross. A strange fire-steel with a waxy finish to pick up the evening glare. At its trigger John's brother, Reid, who had joined us on one other test now, had tied a small cord. The dead leads from old strain gauges were melted into its plastic skin. We stood with it all day, making it fire, and reeling in the heat until our shadows leapt past it.

On a final pull of the cord, a clap, and the end of the white barrel skipped free to jump over the berm ahead. I chased it as it went, clambering up the dirty slope behind. John was pulling another barrel out of the case at his bench as I slid back down to him.

"How did the trip to New York go?" he asked me.

"I was basically congratulated for not being an 'angry white man.'"

"Did you get to meet that guy from the gun markets of Pakistan video?"

"Ha, I did. We didn't really say anything, though. That's one of my favorites."

Reid and I watched as John slotted the next plastic tube into the stubby metal receiver. I was talking about the *Vice* documentary on DD that had just been released.

"We premiered it at a Soho House. Beforehand, an intern took me to a market and said I could get whatever I wanted for lunch."

"Uh-huh."

"I chose a cupcake, which I think unsettled her. I think she was expecting me to eat raw meat and gunpowder."

John pulled his earmuffs back up from his neck. Reid and I took our hands to the sides of our heads.

The crack of the little piece resounded.

We each leaned once again over the awkward shotgun stand, hopeful and expectant, nervous and dubious.

At the end of April I returned to New York and spent a few days at Hod Lipson's invitation in Hell's Kitchen before attending a conference called Inside 3D Printing. I met Andy Greenberg of *Forbes* at a little deli the evening before my talk and told him it was time for him to come to Austin. There was going to be a printed pistol. It was as simple as that.

The keynote speaker at the conference was Abe Reichenthal, the CEO of 3D Systems, who, among other things, assured the prospective investors and industry reps in attendance that printed guns weren't possible and weren't going to happen. The room was half-empty at my own talk, but afterward the TV crews rushed me all the same. In the hour after this, I stayed ringed round with well-wishers and subversives bearing good news. A young man pulled me aside before I left the Javits Center, holding his iPhone below his chest. I leaned in to look at a stringy orange rifle receiver.

"We're printing your lowers in China," he whispered.

He was nodding as I looked up at him.

That night a skinny Jewish girl from Miami took me into Chinatown. I watched her buy a bottle of wine from a corner store encased from the inside with bulletproof glass.

An NBC reporter met me at my hotel in the morning, before I left. It was on my laptop already then, John's latest revision. A file assembly for the pistol. No handle, no trigger. It looked like an old, wheelless gun carriage. She asked if it could fire, and I said yes. I said I'd seen it happen. She asked how it would be made, and I told her on a Stratasys printer. Other people would be able to do it. And then we just sat there for a bit, while she looked at the thing on the laptop and, as her stare faintly shifted, finally past it to something much worse.

At JFK I walked behind a rag on a stick. I thought the back of his jacket read Boomer.

I didn't eat. My writing was sharp and compressed. I stopped calling Ben, Bizzell, or anyone. Instead I prepped the shop, my little closet on Regal Row. On the final day of April I drove up and down 35, crisscrossing the parking lot of the same Home Depot. Behind the trucks for rent I saw thunderclouds to the east and watched them as I crossed Slaughter Creek, dark blue in the late afternoon light. Back south, the road was shimmering in the heat and the cars came over the hill like glossy black beetles. It stormed all through the night, and when I woke, my front door was open.

Back at the gun closet the next evening, the cicadas sang in waves, and everything about me seemed submerged, like in a hot dream. The machine packed the space, enormous and impossible. I sat grimly in my metal chair as the printer's build chamber glowed in the shop like firelight. The print head jittered and skipped, squeezing its thin white paste, as I watched the build through the little window in the door. A sealed pane to separate the phenomenal from every thing-in-itself, angrily slithering in the void like the first forms to creep from calcite seas. We faced each other directly, separated only by a folding end table, as if supplied for the better conducting of our business, our absurd covenant to summon this ghost.

I was flushed from the heat, and my throat clicked. I knew heat like this from when I was a boy. When I worked beneath a red tower in a dirty shirt and steel toes. I was with other boys then, not quite out of high school but already speaking of retirement. They loaded pig lead onto a belt while I climbed the tower to watch the old masters at their furnace. Where it rained lead in Lonoke.

What this printing machine thought of its task, it didn't share. It managed the work briskly behind its little table—or was it mine? I wiped my forehead with my sleeve. Was I watching some silent instruction? Was this some ultimate examination? I feared the questions the beast might ask, those it threatened to answer.

What is man? It demanded.

One of other ideas, I had to admit.

Yes, and time will bear the alternatives.

As the white mass slowly rose on its glistening supports, I thought I saw an old terror the great war planners once had the might, but never the virtue, to try. In the dark, a hostage to the visions of some second godhead, now homeless within my own language, I spoke its name in the very voice of Evil.

REDACTED

The sky was wax paper. The buildings were evanescent behind a single plane of windless heat. On the highway heading north, I watched an Army convoy approach in my rearview. From San Antonio maybe.

"Hey, Becky? Yeah, it's Cody. I think the BBC will want you to come down here."

Road noise. My days were road noise. My dreams.

"That's right, in just a couple of days," I told her.

A friend found me in the tiny shop at the end of the day, babysitting the pistol and snapping its springs. She hurried me to the bar across the street, but I wouldn't look at her when she spoke.

"It's like cheating," I said at last.

My shirt still stuck to my back, and my head ached from the toxic stink of melted plastic. I was filled with an emptying disquiet. Like I'd heard the rumor of war.

I took in the neon of the bar as I spoke again, in words not all that meant for her.

"It's like stealing something from the future. Something that's not yet supposed to be here."

———————

The wind-whipped rain fell when Andy arrived at the closet at Regal Row. He had parked around the corner, unsure of where to find me, and walked to the sagging masonry, and the rusting steel door swung open for him. I sat in the dark on a metal folding chair, letting the pale-blue light flood the space from the gaps between the cardboard and painter's tape covering the windows. The wind picked up and the metal awning wasn't enough to shield us from the spray. Between claps of thunder I asked him to step inside. Flipping the light on, I pulled the handleless door to, and we sat in a cramped corner beneath a fire extinguisher. Andy quickly took in the framed licenses, the gray safe, and the tools and splintered support material scattered across the paint-stained concrete.

"This is it . . . It's incredible how small it is. I mean, that's great."

"Uh, is this a metal detector? This is a metal detector."

I used my chair for a step and plugged the Korean metal detector into a slot in the ceiling beside the fluorescent light. It chirped to life and in the dankness hummed.

"John will be coming after he gets off work," I said.

We drove to the Texican Café, which stood like a counterfeit sale barn. Andy would set up here for his week in town, working beneath the covered patio in front. The waitress took us to a back corner, where we sank into the deep booths in a dim yellow light.

"I have just a few questions to ask since the last time we spoke," Andy said.

I answered the first of these with a tremoring alertness that was quickly spent. Thereafter I stopped looking up.

"I see you describe yourself as a crypto-anarchist now."

I tried to say something about a practical anarchy. About a crypto-anarchy. I tried to say other things.

Andy went on taking notes for a while, and I stared at my plate. "I can't believe there's WiFi," he said, pushing his food to the table's edge. We returned to the warehouse as night settled across the industrial lots.

John and Andy beside the Liberator printer. May 2, 2013.

The light from the open workshop door spilled into the lot, and our shadows walked across the cold metal building beside us. The pistol was disassembled. With our cameras in hand, we leaned in to stare at the sixteen ghostly pieces scattered on the concrete floor. The hammer, pins, and spiraling springs in a coda. Like the shapes of a dead language. A fragmented thought from some other world and beyond any reckoning.

John was prepping primers. We took turns test-firing them in front of the green-lit garage door before the shop. A snap, and sparks flew from the plastic barrel. Andy looked intrigued, and John pried open a burnished cartridge with a pliers to dump the powder on the metal seat of a folding chair. He reached in with a lighter and Andy stepped back. The powder fizzled and spat. We would meet here tomorrow to test.

Early the next morning the heat had broken. A cold, constant wind would last the rest of the day. I grabbed my jacket before I ran out the door to meet Andy and John at the shop. From the gas station beside the Texican, I picked up a yellow nylon cord to run through the loophole we had drawn into the prototype's test trigger. Like the pieces before it, we'd fire it from a stand. After briskly acknowledging each other on Regal Row, we three took our first trip out to Lockhart. The sky was a gray blank the whole way.

We arrived at the chain links of the boundary of the shooting gallery. As we walked down to the berms, the wind ran between us. No one spoke. It was all like countless times before, but with a peculiar morning disorientation. We set up the gun's aluminum stand first, slower and more deliberate than we had ever been before.

From the gun case came the piece, this one without a handle.

A printed panel slid through the trigger guard with threaded bolts on either side to hold it to the cold railing. As it slid on, the metal frame rang. I had seen the plastic .380 work a half dozen times now, but still the white plastic worked its terror on me.

I took a fat brass cartridge from a black-and-gold box. It just slid into the miniature barrel, blurred and melted by acetone vapor from the day before. I saw tiny patches of melted latex from the fingertips of my glove grafted onto the surface, which was slightly yellowed. I slotted the barrel into its groove and twisted it to lock. The fit felt sure enough. Kicking an old steel plate over the frame's feet, I looked over to John, his eyes grinning through his glasses. He was already wearing his earmuffs as he spoke.

"All right. You ready?"

The wind was cutting, and Andy shivered with crossed arms in his checkered shirt. I nodded to John and noted Andy while I took a position behind the frame and to the left. My knee found the dirt. As I fixed my eyes on the space just above the barrel, John gave the count.

"One. Two—"

I pulled the nylon cord.

Crack.

A flash and shrapnel.

I ran to the scaffold.

"Did we make it?" John asked.

I looked back and forth between the barrel and the frame, which read EXP001.

I studied the little barrel's carbon-scored bore, which had survived without flawing. In that dirty pistol gallery I let some of the last nine months catch up to me.

The drive back from Lockhart was quiet. Sensing my anxiety, Andy pressed me.

"So, it seems like you don't really feel a sense of achievement."

"I still have to fire a new one by hand tomorrow. John started another print before we even went out. So, today was at best a prelude, you know?"

I had asked my father to visit. His timing right as ever, he stood outside as we returned to my apartment from the shoot. I wanted him to feel how welcome he was, how grateful I felt, but I was overcome by the sickness of fatigue. That evening we visited a hardware store for the tools to strip the old prototype and clean and prep the new one. One with a handle. One that would be done in the very early morning.

But as the night closed, I could barely stand. At the last moment, even my body became traitorous. Unwilling to reason anymore, I said I'd just chance it. I'd wake up early, hope the print had gone well, and work the pieces together before the film crews arrived.

Before he left me at my apartment, I asked my father, "Can you be there for me tomorrow? I can't do this without your help with the prep."

He drove me back home and told me to save it for the morning. "I'll be there."

I woke in pain, with a jolt. Exhausted. There was a smoky aftertaste in the back of my throat. I ran out the door to take 35 south to the shop. When I arrived to unlock the pocked steel door, the printer remained on, its fans still whirring, and it was bleeding heat. The new pieces were complete on the tray.

By the time my father arrived, I was chipping at the Stratasys trays with a razor. Five pieces cleaned, now six. For forty-five minutes I worked at the hammer body's pin slot. I spat into it and pried with a nail. With other blades we slowly hacked, just avoiding the fleshier plastic of the pistol frame. The film crews would arrive in an hour and a half.

The hunger and fatigue gnawed underneath my eyes and crept to my temples. My legs disappeared from beneath me as I sat. As the rising sun pulsed its warmth and light into the shop, I chipped away at the awkward receiver, my name printed into its side.

In my cap and sunglasses, I moved outside with a folding chair to a spot against the wall of the glass shop next door, picking away the finer pieces of support material still left near the barrel lock. As Becky and Simon of the BBC arrived, my father helped me gather up the three printed barrels and a little pan. As they set up to film, I boiled water in the pan over a camp stove, and over this began heating acetone in a glass jar. Hard case box, egg-crate foam, vapor-treated barrels. I was taking stock.

"All right, Cody. Do you think then you could show us a little of how you make it?" Becky asked.

I brought the little blue laptop at my feet to my knee and pointed at the screen for them. "First," I said, "see that the pistol ██████████████████████.[3] It can be ████████████████ as ██ ████████████, but to print it requires ███████████████████ ██ ███████████████████████. Once the files are ████ ██, depending upon the size of the build envelope, ██████████ ███."

---

[3] These redactions made by demand of the US Department of State.

"Is this how it would work for everyone trying to print it?" Becky asked.

"Well," I began, squinting through the rising sunlight, "on our ███████████████ printer, the ███████████████ ███████████ are printed together with ███████████████. The rest of the pieces can ███████████████ ███████████████████████.

"The selection, orientation, duplication, and placement of ███ ███████████████████ is performed manually, based on the space available on your build tray. It's also necessary to impregnate ███████████████████████████ ███ before manufacturing the other components."

I held a steel cube in my hand. "Liberator receiver steel is manufactured ███████████████████████ ███. The blocks ███████████████████ ███."

"And how do you prepare everything for assembly after it's printed?" asked Simon, who was down on one knee with his camera at his shoulder. His yellow shirt was slightly reflecting on the metal finish of the building beside us.

"After removing most pieces from the build envelope, they can be ███████████████████████, but pieces with ███████████████ ███████████████████████. We use ███████████ ███████ to ███████████████████████ ███████████████████████ ███████████████████████. I estimate that the

frame and the hammer body ███████████
███████████.

"The barrel," I said, holding one up for them from the case I'd earlier prepared. "These must be printed ████ to allow them the ███████████████████████████████████ ███████████████. But an ███████████████ ███████████████. The ███████████████ ███████████████ ███████████████. Liberator barrel bores must be ████ ███████████████ in a pretty lengthy process. It took me a few hours to really get the feel for it."

I was pointing to the ███████████ now.

"I ███████████████████████████████████, placing that ███████████████████████████████████ ███████████████, being careful in how ████ ███████████████. The ███████ is gently ████ ████, which in turn ███████████████████. Once I see ███████████████████████████████████ ███████████████. But this is not enough for ████ ███████████."

I went on.

"I allow one ███████████████████████ ███████████, then ███████████████████████ ███████████████████████████████████. This encourages ███████████████. Once the barrel has ████ ███████████████, it must be ███████████ ███████████████████████████████████ ███████████████████████████████. This is a

critical step, because ███████████████████████████
██
██████████████████████████████████."

They were transfixed around me, seated as I was in my hot metal chair. I began to assemble the pistol for them.

"First you drop the ████████████████████████████████
████████ into the ██████████████████████████████. You can then ███████████████████████████████ with some pressure applied to ███████████████████. The hammer subassembly is ████████████ ████████████████████████████████, and ██████████████████ ████████████████████. The springs are ████████████████████ ████████████████████████████████████ and ██████████████ ██ ██████████████."

I flipped the whitened piece over in my hand. It was hard to look at directly in the sun.

"This next assembly ████████████████████████████████ ██████████ by inserting ██████████████████. These ██████ are ██████████ and must ████████████████████████████. After ██████████████████████ the hammer and the trigger ██████ you add the ████████████████████████████ ████████████████████████████████. At this point ████████████████ ██ ██."

I looked up at each of them through my glasses to see if they followed or were trying to get in any questions.

"The firing pin for the pistol is actually ███████████████ ██████████████████████████. This nail is ████████████████████ ████████████ and ████████████████████████████████████."

I pushed it in with my finger.

"And at last, you take your barrel and ███████████████." I did this while still looking up, ██████ the barrel with my right hand and slightly exaggerating the effort involved.

"This is the Liberator pistol."

It was here.

At last Andy arrived, and we all drove out together.

Closer to Lockhart, the elevated highways heaved into view. Though It was shut up in its box, I could sense it. And as the suspended freeways began to look like the naked gunwales of some monstrous and decomposing ship, I was unsure just who was driving the car. The dogs followed us as we rolled into the woods outside the old shooting gallery in Lockhart, and It made its way from my front seat to a table out on the dirt.

They set their cameras up slowly and faced the same cracking berms we'd caught in our phones' recordings too many times to count. It was placed on a stanchioned shelf, which looked out to the rusting plates here used for targets, and It traveled at last to my hand. With little ceremony, I staggered my legs, looked down, and looked up.

And like that it happened.

And maybe it wasn't supposed to, or shouldn't have been possible. Or maybe only when it had happened did it even become possible. But no one talked about that then.

Andy chuckled in disbelief, soon walking off to scroll through the pictures on his camera. My father congratulated me. The BBC team asked if I'd like to try it again, but I moved to the shade of a blue canopy at the center of the gallery to take questions. The sun was in my eyes, and my thoughts were uncollected, but I saw some things more clearly then. Becky asked what it felt like to shoot It, like I wasn't the one being wielded for the last nine months, and like It didn't speak for itself. She asked about world governments and policy responses, while It sat in its open box on the stand in the midday sun, silently laughing at the both of us.

Later on, Simon was practicing shooting with a black rifle we'd brought. When he had had his fun, he called Becky to come over and give it a try. But she'd have none of it.

"Aw, Becky, now . . . ," he said.

My father and Simon offered differing explanations, when at last it was clear she wouldn't shoot.

"Maybe she thinks it would be too much like endorsing your message."

"She's just being a bad sport! Come on, Becks!"

I spoke up from the shade. "She thinks it will leave a stain. Morally. She thinks she'll lose her innocence."

And she would have. But I had found mine.

Hours later, when I had returned to my apartment, a trio of filmmakers brought takeout for dinner. They sat around and behind me with their cameras as I finished the video I would put on YouTube at midnight: an announcement that the file was online and free to download. It was brief. Just a few clips of a sunrise and some bombers. "Download today."

A cameraman asked me what would happen if the government stepped in tomorrow.

"You can't plan for good luck like that. But if power did step in, it would guarantee the outcome, wouldn't it? Something like the Streisand effect."

The file was uploaded and ready to share. The link was in a draft email I had prepared to send to Haroon. So, this was the Wiki

Weapon, I thought. The blood physible. It would be received like a signal, I thought. Not of a constructive but of an absolute disorder. A signal of the world as it is.

In an hour I had a call to announce the drop to the BBC during the morning commute, and there were four words on my mind.

I pressed Send.

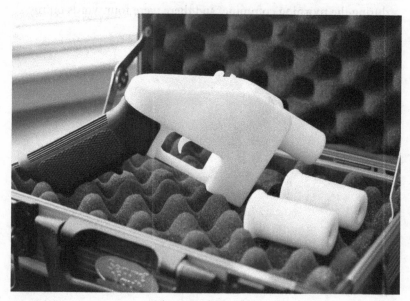

Liberator Pistol, May 2013.

Nine Months of Night

On a late summer's evening, 2012, the sky over the blacklands was blasted red brass. The color of catastrophe. Dallas had released me south through her great gates and to the flaring evening, where, exposed on a broad plain, I caravanned with the dusty Fords and swaying tractor-trailers. We were each the silent, bronze subjects of an immense and setting sun. Out in the brush beyond was a familiar feeling, one I'd spent weekends chasing in college. Past the trucker haunts littering I-40, and out past the browned and browning concrete of Arkadelphia and Prescott, I'd find it. In the somewheres south of Texarkana the tar lines would begin to shimmer.

Before Waco I exited the interstate unconsciously, rolling to a ruined heap of a gas station. A pale sign with double chevrons was posted above. Filling up, I leaned against the car and turned slowly to mark it overhead: the recycled ordinary of every failed order; a standing valentine to history, to a world that could still be made safe—for anything. Some impossible ghost shambling out of the desert of another epoch would take this place for one of arms.

Leaving, I watched the sign in the mirror. Its stale flicker, in red and white and blue, would struggle tonight to beat back the wrathful blackness galloping from the east. The dusk reminded me of promises I'd have to keep, and I sped again into the night.